Chosen by THE TIMES's Music Critic as his "Book of the Year" (1968)
"Wholeheartedly recommendable" *The Times*

"Original and stimulating ... the most lucid attempt I have yet read to explain the reasons for the continuing compulsive fascination of Wagner's music over friend and foe alike" *Music and Musicians*

"Brilliantly fascinating" *BBC Radio*
"Excellent . . . conspicuous for two virtues that Wagner lacked, brevity and lucidity" *Times Literary Supplement*

"Short but splendidly meaty" *New Statesman*
"Includes more thinking in its 112 pages than most authors expend in a lifetime . . . every essay in this book abounds in perception" *Opera News*

"Fresh, individual, intelligent" *Sunday Times*
"To be read by every operagoer, whether he be a Wagnerian or not" *Opera*

Also in Panther Books

The Memoirs of Berlioz Edited and translated by David Cairns
Mozart Alfred Einstein
Schubert Alfred Einstein
Handel Newman Flower
The Joy of Music Leonard Bernstein

Bryan Magee

Aspects of Wagner

PANTHER
GRANADA PUBLISHING
London Toronto Sydney New York

Published by Granada Publishing Limited
in Panther Books 1972
Reprinted 1978

ISBN 0 586 03774 8

First published in Great Britain by
Alan Ross 1968
Copyright © Bryan Magee 1968

Granada Publishing Limited
Frogmore, St Albans, Herts AL2 2NF
and
3 Upper James Street, London W1R 4BP
1221 Avenue of the Americas, New York, NY10020, USA
117 York Street, Sydney, NSW 2000, Australia
100 Skyway Avenue, Toronto, Ontario, Canada M9W 3A6
Trio City, Coventry Street, Johannesburg 2001, South Africa
CML Centre, Queen & Wyndham, Auckland 1, New Zealand

Made and printed in Great Britain by
C. Nicholls & Company Ltd
The Philips Park Press, Manchester
Set in Monotype Garamond

Contents

To Bernard Williams

One

Wagner's Theory of Opera

Lohengrin, the most often performed of Wagner's operas, was finished in 1847, when he was 34. From then until the age of 40, when he began the music for *The Ring*, he composed nothing at all – the only such gap in his creative life. What he did instead, having developed to its limits the form of German Romantic opera he had inherited, was carry out a complete reappraisal of it. This was done, characteristically, in public, in a series of books, most of them written between 1848 and 1851. The most important were *The Work of Art of the Future* (1849), *Opera and Drama* (1850–1851) and *A Message to My Friends* (1851). They embodied an entirely new theory of opera, which he then went on to realize in his remaining works: *The Ring*, *Tristan and Isolde*, *The Mastersingers* and *Parsifal*.

This is a unique phenomenon. Here was a great artist theorizing about his art in volume after volume of published prose, and then going on to embody the theories in creative masterpieces. We should say it was all too self-conscious and synthetic, did not the works themselves refute this. Some

writers have asserted that the practice is quite different from the theory and independent of it, but no
one can seriously maintain that who has actually read
the books, where over and again the subsequent practice of Wagner's greatest works is elaborated. (I can
only assume that these writers are tacitly and hope-
fully justifying themselves for not having read them.
Wagner's theories are constantly being described as
nonsense by people who do not know what they
are.)

I must say, though, that anyone who wants to
avoid reading his prose has my sympathy. He writes
like an autodidact, with flowery expressions, a voca-
bulary intended to impress, unnecessary abstractions
and elaborate sentence structures. (These faults are
compounded in the nineteenth-century English
translation, by Ashton Ellis: when Bernard Shaw
called this "a masterpiece of interpretation and an
eminent addition to our literature" his usual critical
acumen had been given a day off. In this book I
have attempted my own translations.) One forms the
conviction that the prose was improvised, poured
out without forethought or discipline – that when
Wagner embarked on each individual sentence he
had no idea how it was going to end. Many pas-
sages are intolerably boring. Some do not mean anything at all. It always calls for sustained effort from
the reader to pick out meaning in the cloud of
words. Often one has to go on reading for several

pages before beginning to descry, like solid figures in a mist, what it is he is saying.

No doubt there are many reasons for this, but I think the chief is that new things were beginning to form inside him which he was trying to articulate as a theoretical system when all the time their unconscious, autonomous development was towards works of art, namely the later operas. In other words I think that although the operas correspond with the theory, and were produced after the theory, it was the theory that was derived from the operas rather than the other way round. Something Wagner said many years later confirms this: the attitude of mind in which he had written his theoretical works had been, he said, an abnormal one because it had driven him "to treat as an intellectual theory something that my creative intuition already had an assured grasp of". Even allowing for probable exaggeration of his former assurance, it explains the fact that has puzzled so many people, that operas so deeply felt should embody pre-existing theories, and that the one which embodies them completely, *Tristan*, should be the most passionately and spontaneously composed of all.

Wagner's theory of opera is interesting on many levels – for itself, and as the most important contribution to the subject by a great composer, and for the light it throws on his own works. One of the most fruitful and influential books on opera to be

published in our own time – *Opera as Drama* by
Joseph Kerman, published in 1956 – begins with the
words: "I make no apology for the Wagnerian title.
This book is far from Wagnerian, but the point of
view it develops is really the basic one celebrated by
Opera and Drama, that astonishing volume of a hundred years ago. . . ."

I shall try now to give a clear exposition of Wagner's theory. And because Wagner's writing is so
little conducive to quotation I shall put it largely in
my own words.

The highest point ever reached in human creative
achievement was Greek tragedy. This is for five
main reasons, which should be considered together.
First, it represented a successful combination of the
arts – poetry, drama, costumes, mime, instrumental
music, dance, song – and as such had greater scope
and expressive powers than any of the arts alone.
Second, it took its subject matter from myth, which
illuminates human experience to the depths, and in
universal terms. "The unique thing about myth is
that it is true for all time; and its content, no matter
how terse or compact, is inexhaustible for every
age." Third, both the content and the occasion of
performance had religious significance. Fourth, it
was a religion of "the purely human", a celebration
of life – as in the marvellous chorus in the *Antigone*
of Sophocles which begins

Numberless are the world's wonders, but none
More wonderful than man. . . .

Fifth, the entire community took part.

This art-form was ideal because it was all-embracing: its expressive means embraced all the arts, its subject matter embraced all human experience, and its audience embraced the whole population. It was the summation of living.

But with the passage of time it disintegrated. The arts all went their separate ways and developed alone – instrumental music without words, poetry without music, drama without either, and so on. In any case its available content dissolved when Greek humanism was superseded by Christianity, a religion which divided man against himself, teaching him to look on his body with shame, his emotions with suspicion, sensuality with fear, sexual love with feelings of guilt. This life, it taught, was a burden, this world a vale of tears, our endurance of which would be rewarded at death, which was the gateway to eternal bliss. In effect this religion was, as it was bound to be, anti-art. The alienation of man from his own nature, especially his emotional nature; the all-pervading hypocrisy to which this gave rise throughout the Christian era; the devaluation of life and the world and hence, inevitably, their wonderfulness; the conception of man as being not a god but a worm, and a guilty one at that; all this is pro-

foundly at odds with the very nature and existence
of art. Such a religion, based as it is on the celebration of death and on hostility to the emotions, repu-
diates both the creative impulse and its subject
matter. Art is the celebration of life, and the exploration of life in all its aspects. If life is unimportant –
merely a diminutive prelude to the real Life which
is to begin with death – then art can be only of negli-
gible importance too.

The descent from the Greek achievement had
reached rock bottom by the nineteenth century.
Theatrical performance had degenerated from being
a religious occasion in which the entire community
took part to being entertainment for tired business
men and their wives. It was frivolous, often to the
point of contentlessness, and such values as it embodied were those of the Christian-bourgeois society
around it. The most frivolous, vulgar, socially
exclusive and contentless of all theatrical forms was
opera. Its conventions were grotesque, its plots ridiculous, its libretti fatuous. Yet none of this was
thought to matter, neither by its audiences nor its
creators, for these things were there only to provide
a framework for stage spectacle, catchy tunes and
vocal display by star singers. Even so, opera was
potentially the greatest of the arts, for it alone in the
modern world could combine all the others, as
Greek tragedy had done. What was needed, therefore, was a revolution in opera that would turn it

into the comprehensive art-form it was capable of becoming, in which all the resources of drama, poetry, instrumental music, song, acting, gesture, costumes and scenery would once more combine in the theatrical presentation of myth to an audience of all the people. The subject matter of such works, though purely human, would be the deepest things of life. Far from being mere entertainment, therefore, they would be almost religious enactments.

This, in a nutshell, was the Wagnerian programme. It was not based just on the slogan "*Back to Greek tragedy*!", for it looked forward to a new and better way of doing what the Greeks had done – better, because it would draw on resources which the Greeks had not had. Shakespeare, "a genius the like of which was never heard of", had developed poetic drama beyond anything the Greeks could have conceived. Beethoven had developed the expressive powers of music beyond the limits of speech altogether, even the speech of a Shakespeare. The artist of the future (no marks for guessing who) would combine the achievements of Shakespeare and Beethoven in a single art form, something which, on the analogy of poetic drama, might be called music drama.

How would music drama differ from existing opera and existing drama? Traditional drama depicts, for the most part, what goes on outside people, specifically what goes on *between* them. Its stuff is personal relationships. As for what goes on inside them, almost its only concern here is with their motives. Dramatic development is a chain of cause and effect, one motivated action bringing about or conflicting with another, the whole adding up to a self-contained interlocking system that constitutes the plot. This requires that the forces which act on the characters be convincingly shown, and this in turn requires that they be placed in their social and political context, and their interaction with it articulated. The more motive is explored and displayed, the more "political" the play has to be – the plays of Shakespeare conjure up whole courts and governments and armies, ruling classes, city states, feuding families and the rest, with a vividness which would be unbelievable had he not done it, and always in terms of warmly alive individuals.

Music drama would be the opposite of this in almost every respect. It would be about the insides of the characters. It would be concerned with their emotions, not their motives. It would explore and articulate the ultimate reality of experience, what goes on in the heart and the soul. This had been made possible by Beethoven, who had developed in music the power to express inner reality in all its fullness, unfettered by the limitations of language with its dependence on the use of specific concepts and its permeation by the laws of logic. In this kind of drama the externals of plot and social relationships would be reduced to a minimum. Its chief requirement was for situations which remained unchanged long enough for the characters' full inner experience of them, and response to them, to be expressed. Myth was ideal for this, because it dealt in archetypal situations and because its universal validity, regardless of time and place, meant that the dramatist could almost dispense with a social and political context and present, as it were "pure", the inner drama.

Music drama would also be the reverse of traditional opera, for in traditional opera the drama was merely a framework on which to hang the music – drama was the means, music the end – whereas the object of music drama was the presentation of archetypal situations *as experienced by the participants*, and to this dramatic end music was a means, albeit a uniquely expressive one.

Among the actual music dramas which Wagner went on to write, *The Mastersingers* is an exception to these rules on many counts, all springing from the fact that it was about the one and only subject that he regarded as of fundamental importance yet "political", namely the artist's relations to his art, and hence to tradition, and hence to society. Alone of the music dramas it is located in historical time and place – sixteenth-century Nuremberg – and has ordinary

human beings as characters, one of whom, Hans
Sachs, was a historical personage. Alone among
Wagner's works it is a comedy, and the extraversion
of its expressive language corresponds to this fact
and to the "political" subject: the verse lines are
longer than in the previous works, and rhyme con-
ventionally, and contain stanzaic songs, while the
music is altogether more diatonic, and in predomi-
nantly major keys. But the orchestra still performs
the same function of articulating the existential
drama, the flow of life and feeling inwardly experienced by the characters. The harmony with which
inner and outer worlds are woven together creates a
sense of wellbeing which pervades the whole work.
The context is warmly and exclusively human, and
yet the subject, though not mythical, had a quasi-
religious significance for Wagner, and was intended
to have so for the audience. The audience being
addressed is very much the "folk", the whole
community.

   Tristan and Isolde was the work which, by a
general agreement which includes Wagner's, embodied his theories more or less to perfection. Of its
composition he was to write: "Here I sank myself
with complete confidence into the depths of the
soul's inner workings, and then built outwards from
this, the world's most intimate and central point,
towards external forms. This explains the brevity of
the text, which you can see at a glance. For whereas

a writer whose subject matter is historical has to use so much circumstantial detail to keep the continuity of his action clear on the surface that it impedes his exposition of more inward themes, I trusted myself to deal solely with these latter. Here life and death and the very existence and significance of the external world appear only as manifestations of the inner workings of the soul. The dramatic action itself is nothing but a response to that inmost soul's requirements, and it reaches the surface only insofar as it is pushed outwards from within."

What Wagner thought he had done above all else was develop an art form which made possible the expression, and hence the experience, of unbounded feeling about specific things – what he called "the emotionalizing of the intellect". Beethoven, the first composer to proclaim his inner conflicts, had developed in music the power to articulate the inmost drama of the psyche, but because his expressive means were confined to those of absolute music he could give utterance only to generalized emotions: he could not be specific without resorting to words. His needs drove him in this direction, therefore, and in the last movement of his last symphony he introduced, for the first time, poetry. It was this combination of poetry and symphony that provided the take-off point for Wagner. He recognized that Beethoven's use of it had not been very successful, but he never ceased to acknowledge it as the starting point of his own work. When he laid the foundation stone of his own theatre at Bayreuth, on his fifty-ninth birthday, he marked the occasion with a performance of this work which was, in a sense, the foundation stone of his art. It was the Choral symphony that had shown him that the symphony orchestra, with its language deeper than words but unspecific, could be combined with the human voice to provide a complex means of expression which used words and had all their advantages without being subject to their limitations. His own contribution was to bring this language into the theatre and use it as a means of dramatic expression with depths of utterance inaccessible to the Greeks, inaccessible even to Shakespeare.

Like Beethoven's music, Wagner's was symphonic, that is to say an organized structure consisting of themes and their development. But whereas in Beethoven's symphonies the course taken by the music – the exposition of the themes, their relative keys, their development and their recapitulation – followed the requirements of sonata form, in Wagner's operas it followed the requirements of the drama. It did so on several levels at once, and technically the process was a complicated one. But a single aspect of it can be used by way of illustration to cast some light on the rest.

If, says Wagner, he writes a line like "Liebe giebt

Lust zum Leben" (Love gives delight to living) the concepts involved are obviously consonant and therefore no change of key is called for. But suppose the line is "Liebe bringt Lust und Leid" (Love brings delight and sorrow) then delight and sorrow are opposites and the music should modulate between them. What should happen is that the key in which the phrase begins on the word "love" should remain the same through "delight" and then change on the word "sorrow". But the modulation must express the interrelationship of delight and sorrow in the state of love, at the same time as their difference; it must articulate their conditioning of each other. (This, said Wagner, was something words could not do, only music.) Now suppose the next line is "Doch in ihr Weh webt sie auch Wonnen" (which might be very freely translated: "Yet even its pain gives us joy"). Then the key of "sorrow" from the end of the previous line should be carried through as far as "pain", because the emotional mood remains the same. But then the verb in this second line starts a shift of the mood back towards that of the first half of the previous line; therefore the music should begin to change key on "gives", and on the word "joy" should arrive back at the key of "Love gives delight".

Now this is just a very simple example involving two lines and two keys. In their long monologues or narratives Wagner's characters set all sorts of feel-

ings and ideas and incidents and other characters
in conflict, conjure up disparate memories, consider
various alternatives, make decisions, change their
minds; and the music modulates with them through
multifarious and remote keys, giving subtlest musical expression to all these interrelationships, and
above all revealing their underlying relationship to
the primary key associated with the basic emotional
mood of the episode.

Modulation, again, is only one of the elements in
music, and Wagner absorbed all of them into the
syntax of his dramatic language. The result was a
symphonic web of infinite plasticity, moving freely
in response to whatever was being done and said on
the stage – which alone determined whether a new
theme was introduced or an old one repeated, the
guises they appeared in and the way they were
developed: whether the music modulated or stayed
in the same key, threw up a single melody or rami-
fied into contrapuntal lines. This is what Wagner
meant when he talked of putting music at the service
of drama, of music being the means and drama the
end. It is the opposite of opera as an excuse for
music and spectacle – the traditional opera which,
even if dramatically continuous, was always musi-
cally discontinuous, a series of self-contained "numbers" of entirely unsymphonic character in which
the orchestra was used chiefly as "accompaniment".

To listen to Wagner's music simply as music,

without regard to the words or the drama, is to miss all this. It is to abstract the music from a very much larger but still single medium of expression – verbal-musical-dramatic – of which it is less than the whole. The music is so good that it is easy to do this and lose sight of what one misses. But how much one does miss astonishes those who, after half a lifetime of enjoying the music, for the first time study the texts and see the operas in performance.

Wagner's central theory is fed by numberless tributary theories, each of which is argued out at length, either in context in one of the books or in a pamphlet or article to itself: how the mass of the people came to be dissociated from art; the commercialization of culture; the history of opera and its decay; what political and social changes were needed before a comprehensive art form would again be possible; the strain of civilization; the relationship of the artist to society – and myth in its relation to both; symbolism; the reasons why speech alone is inadequate as a means of expression; the relationship between words and music; the development of symphonic music, and its application to drama; the different expressive powers not only of music and poetry but, within music, of harmony and melody, orchestra and voice. Some of the most illuminating discussions are among the most technical: the connection between key structure and poetic content; the reasons why the most appropriate verse form is characterized by short lines and alliteration.

On every one of these subjects, and many more, Wagner has interesting, important and frequently original things to say. On Beethoven he is outstandingly perceptive. His criticisms of traditional opera, though self-interested, are of lasting value. He had deep insight into the nature of symbolism (he was, of course, the acknowledged progenitor of the Symbolist Movement in French poetry). He had the most remarkable understanding, long before psychology or anthropology, of the psychic import of myth. He realized half a century before Freud that "today we have only to interpret the Oedipus myth in a way that keeps faith with its essential meaning to get a coherent picture from it of the whole history of mankind. . . ." The essentials of modern psychology seem to be present, unco-ordinated, in his writings.

Although, as we have seen, Wagner's belief that the ultimate realities were those of inward experience led him to set a low value on political and social content in drama, we have also seen that he regarded widespread political changes in the world outside the theatre as necessary if art was again to occupy its rightful place as the focal point of man's life in society. So he was, as a young man, passionately interested in politics. Indeed he was an active revolutionary. All the theoretical works we have been considering were written in political exile, an exile which lasted for twelve years. They contain many echoes, in both ideas and phraseology, from the writings of Karl Marx up to and including *The Communist Manifesto*, which had just appeared in 1848. But Wagner's concern was not political economy, it was art – his real objection to existing society was that it was bad for art. His disgust with industrialism and the bourgeois hegemony, and their alliance with the Christian churches, and the way they degraded art to the level of entertainment, and turned most of the population into wage slaves cut off from everything that made life worth living, drove him to take an active part in the Dresden rising of 1849 along with his friend Michael Bakunin, the most famous of anarchists. The text of *The Ring*, which he wrote in the years immediately following, contains a great deal of political symbolism of a Liberal-cum-Marxist kind. (Bernard Shaw's book *The Perfect Wagnerite* is a detailed interpretation of it as a Marxist allegory.) By the time he came to write the music his views about the desirability of political symbolism in opera had changed. But it is probable that the original model for Siegfried was Bakunin.

Viewed as a whole, Wagner's theories have major faults. One is their political naïveté and utopianism, characteristic of their time and place. Another is their romantic idealization of Greece – also charac-

teristic of their time and place, having been given a
dominating position in German thought by Lessing,
Goethe, Schiller and Hölderlin, and then powerfully
stimulated by Byron. A third is their historicism.
The only way Wagner seems able to discuss anything is in historical terms. If he wants to advocate
something, anything, he has to demonstrate that it
once existed, describe how it worked, account for its
decline, and then call for a return to it. This means
that three-quarters of any argument from his pen is
likely to be clothed in bogus history. To some subsequent critics the arguments have been not merely
clothed but hidden – they have been under the illusion that when they had refuted the history they had
refuted the argument. But this is not so. An argument can be illuminating, and indeed valid, even
though couched in false historical terms.

A more serious, if more elusive, objection is that
there is something passive about it all – and also
something solipsistic, the two being related. By
filleting drama of motive and presenting it almost
entirely in terms of emotional response Wagner
shows things acting on people but not people
acting on things. Their feelings in relation to situations and each other are poured out in unparalleled
fullness, but this very fact means that the situation
itself, or the relationship, is somehow "given". We
see the characters almost entirely from the inside –
very little as active in the world, motivating events,

assuming control of situations and changing them. The only kind of responsibility they ever seem to take is the passive one of acknowledging necessity. Wagner's recipe is for a drama which consists not of actions but of reactions. His characters are subjects only of feeling: of action they are always the objects. One can go even farther and say that his main characters are victims: Tristan and Isolde obviously so, but also Wotan, who, in spite of being ruler of the Gods, is from the very beginning of *The Ring* at the mercy of forces he is powerless to control, and in the end he and all the gods are destroyed by them. Siegfried, though supposed to be the supreme hero, never at any time understands his situation, and is always the puppet of his own ignorance, which in the end destroys him. Wagner's last opera, *Parsifal*, passes beyond even this emotional passivity and is concerned with complete renunciation.

Solipsism is suggested by the fact that reality for Wagner is always to be found in the psyche, not in the external world. Inner emotion is so overwhelmingly experienced that everything else, including other people, has only a shadowy existence on its periphery. Wagner's characters do not seem really to relate to each other: the being of each is, as it were, a sphere of passionate feeling that reveals its interior to the audience but only its surface to the other characters. It has been said of *The Ring* that in the deepest sense there is only one character, the different "characters" being aspects of a single personality, so that the work is a portrait of the psyche as well as a depiction of the world.

But for all its shortcomings Wagner's theory was the first to seize on the truth about the place of great music in opera and its relationship to the drama; and it is still, after a hundred years, at the centre of opera theory in general. It even has significance beyond opera: for instance it illuminates the function of poetry in Shakespeare's plays. One way or another it informs most serious discussion of the drama today. And its effect on the world of music would be hard to overestimate. As Edward J. Dent wrote in his book *Opera*: "Wagner, through his writings and through his own personal influence, has converted the musical world, or a good part of it, to something like a new outlook on music in general. It may be that he was mistaken in supposing that the modern world could ever recover the attitude of ancient Greece to the religious aspect of musical drama, but he certainly induced it to take music, and especially opera, far more seriously than it had ever done before."

Two

Jews — Not Least in Music

In the last hundred years three people have produced theories about man and his environment which in depth, originality and scope are equal to almost any before them – Marx, Freud and Einstein. The theories are not compatible, but each is a creative achievement of the highest order, and their influence has been immense. Marx, in fact, has had more influence in less time than anyone else in history: within a mere seventy years of his death a third of the human race was living under governments calling themselves Marxist. The intellectual achievement of Einstein is more impressive, and may prove in the end to be as important in its practical application, if only because of the hydrogen bomb. As for Freud, he has done more to extend our vision inward, into ourselves, than anyone else; doing his work required unimaginable courage, and unlike that of the other two its good consequences are more obvious than its bad. All three, I think, must be ranked among the greatest of the world's creative geniuses.

All three were Jews. This fact is remarkable for

many reasons. One is that there had been only one
Jew of comparable achievement, Spinoza, in the
previous eighteen hundred years. Another is that, in
spite of this, these three pioneered a Jewish renaissance of fantastic proportions. Jewish philosophers
since Marx include Bergson, Husserl, Wittgenstein
and Popper. Not only Freud but most of the famous
psychoanalysts have been Jews: in the sciences not
only Einstein but Nobel Prize winners so numerous
it would be tedious to list them (since the Nobel
Prize began in 1901 it has been awarded to more
than forty Jews). All this is doubly amazing when
one remembers that the total number of Jews in the
world is only about thirteen million – the population
of Greater London.

In no field has their contribution been more outstanding than in music. Mahler was Jewish, as were
Schoenberg and most of his famous pupils. The greatest instrumentalists of this century have been Jews.
Even if one forgets Kreisler, Schnabel and all the
other great dead, and considers only the living, the
best violinists are nearly all Jews (and, oddly enough,
from Russia) – Heifetz, Menuhin, Stern, Milstein,
Zukerman, Perlman, Oistrakh. Jewish pianists include Gilels, Serkin, Rubinstein, Solomon, Horo-
witz, Ashkenazy, Boman, Perahia, Ax and Baren-
boim. And the conductors Solti, Bernstein, Orman-
dy, Dorati, Levine, Previn and Maazel. These lists,
themselves grossly incomplete, can not be matched

by the $99\frac{1}{2}$ per cent of the human race who are not
Jews. If anyone wants to tell me this is coincidence
my reply is that this is simply not credible. The intellectual and artistic output of Jews in this century
relative to their numbers is a phenomenon for which
I can think of no parallel in history since Athens
five centuries before Christ. It is something that calls
for explanation.

In fact there are two questions requiring an answer, each of which helps to set the other. First, why
in the modern era did Jews produce scarcely any
creative work of the front rank until only the last
century? Second, why was there then this amazing
harvest of achievement? Jews tend naturally to be
much more excited by the second question than the
first. I have often heard them discuss it and often discussed it with them. The trouble with the answers
they must commonly produce is that they fail to
accommodate the facts behind the first question.

One explanation, offered with extreme reluctance
to a non-Jew (and for that reason, I am sure, much
more commonly believed than expressed), is that
Jews are specially gifted in some innate way. People
who think this are really just reformulating the
ancient doctrine of the "chosen people" in terms of
genetics. There is no evidence for its truth. German
and American racists have tried very hard in our
century to produce scientific evidence for this kind
of difference between races, and always failed. Jews,

of all people, ought by now to be prejudiced against Master Race theories. But perhaps that is asking too much of human nature. One's natural reaction to disparagement is to assert one's special value, and centuries of persecution can only have given the Chosen People doctrine added appeal. Nevertheless the belief by people of any race that they are inherently superior is beneath respect, and I have no hesitation in saying of this one, as of the others, that it is superstitious, obviously false, and nasty. Most Jews, I am sure, do not believe it.

The explanation most commonly offered is that the cultural distinction of modern Jewry is due to their unique religious and intellectual tradition. But what this implies is the exact opposite of the truth. For it is only Jews who have escaped from their religious and intellectual tradition who have achieved greatness. Every single Jew I can think of who has reached the highest levels of attainment in the modern era has repudiated Judaism: Spinoza, Heine and Mendelssohn if anyone wants to include them, Marx, Disraeli, Freud, Mahler, Einstein, Trotsky, Kafka, Wittgenstein, Schoenberg.* So it seems, rather, that freedom from that most tribal, observance-ridden and past-oriented of religions is a precondition of true and deep originality.

* Schoenberg returned publicly to the faith in 1933, but made it clear that this was not a religious conversion but a declaration of solidarity with the Jews in face of Nazi persecution.

And here we come to what seems to me the right explanation – and one that answers the first as well as the second of our two questions. Originality in fundamentals is inimical to any closed, authoritarian culture, because such cultures do not and can not allow their basic assumptions to be questioned. The two greatest moralists there have ever been, Socrates and Jesus, were executed for doing precisely this. Only in comparative freedom – or at least when authority was on the defensive – has individual creativeness flourished: in ancient Greece, the Renaissance, Protestant Europe, or the rest of Europe since the dawn of liberal thought. Authoritarian cultures – ancient Rome, classical China and India, medieval Christendom, contemporary Communism – have been by comparison barren. Of course they have had their brilliant lawgivers, scholars, theologians, establishment artists and so on *within the system*, but any man who denied the basic assumptions of the system itself was crushed – in most cases tortured and killed. In such circumstances radical innovation is impossible.

The great flowering of European drama, poetry, science, mathematics, philosophy, music, began with the emancipation of these activities from the Church. Not surprisingly it took two or three generations to reach full growth. So the peak came in the seventeenth century (though music, as always, was behind the others – just as, later, the high point of

Romanticism in music came when the Romantic Movement in literature was already spent). There could have been no question of its happening within the Church. Some of the greatest geniuses of all, like Copernicus and Galileo, had their work officially condemned by the Church. The Inquisition which tried Galileo had thousands of less eminent intellectuals imprisoned, tortured or executed. In Italy scientific work was stamped out altogether and did not revive for generations.

But in all this the Jews had little part – except in Spain, where they were treated in a way that foreshadowed the Nazis. Over most of Europe they were still living in a closed religious culture of their own, where they were condemned to remain until the ghettoes were opened. The banning of instrumental music and graven images from the Synagogue meant that within that culture the development of the non-literary arts was just as impossible as the development of science. And when the ghettoes were finally opened the Jews had a parallel renaissance of their own, with all the same broad features: the lapse of two or three generations between emancipation and the peak of achievement; the dissociation of the greatest creative geniuses from the closed religious and intellectual tradition; the lifelong struggle against institutional prejudice and personal resentment – and, before the end, murder on an enormous scale, highly organized and state-supported.

If this explanation is the right one the Jewish renaissance was a once-for-all phenomenon which can neither continue nor happen again. As time goes on the difference between Jews and non-Jews is bound to diminish. Now that most Jews, like most other Westerners, have abandoned religion the chief thing that gives them any active sense of being Jewish is anti-Semitism, above all the recent attempt to murder them all. Orthodox Jews dread and hate integration, but they are a minority, and now that the taboo on intermarriage has weakened for all but a few it is bound to happen in the long run.

And what, it may be asked, has all this to do with Wagner? The answer is that he was the first person to see any of it – a small part, perhaps, but as much as it was possible for anyone in the nineteenth century to do, and more than anyone else in that century did. And because of his anti-Semitism he has never been given credit for it. The Jewish renaissance has happened almost entirely since his day, and he did not foresee it, but he did regard the fact that there had been no great Jewish composers up to his time as something requiring explanation. The explanation he offered was almost unbelievably original, and largely correct. The key document is an article he published in 1850 called *Das Judentum in der Musik* (Judaism in Music). Its central argument is as follows.

A really great creative artist is one who, in freely

expressing his own fantasies, needs, aspirations and conflicts, articulates those of a whole society. This is made possible by the fact that, through his earliest relationships, mother tongue, upbringing and all his first experience of life, the cultural heritage on which he has entered at birth is woven into the whole fabric of his personality. He has a thousand roots in it of which he is unaware, nourishing him below the level of consciousness, so that when he speaks for himself he quite unconsciously speaks for others. Now in Wagner's time it was impossible for a Jewish artist to be in this position. The ghettoes of Western Europe had only begun to be opened in the wake of the French Revolution, and their abolition was going on throughout the nineteenth century. The Jewish composers of Wagner's day were among the very first emancipated Jews, pastless in the society in which they were living and working. They spoke its language with, literally, a foreign accent. In composing its music – including, quite often, Church music – they were turning their backs on a distinctive and entirely different musical tradition of their own. So their art could not possibly be "the conscious and proclaimed unconscious", which Wagner believed all great art to be. It could only be synthesized at the upper levels of the personality. In fact its articulated content could originate no deeper than the composer's conscious intentions. So however great his gifts it could only be shallow by the standards of great art. "Mendelssohn", Wagner wrote, "has shown us that a Jew can have the richest abundance of specific talents, be a man of the broadest yet most refined culture, of the loftiest, most impeccable integrity, and yet not be able – not even once, with the help of all these qualities – to produce in us that deep, heart-seizing, soul-searching experience that we expect from art."

One does not need to share Wagner's view of Mendelssohn to see that this argument is substantially correct. The obvious thing about it that Wagner failed to see is that of its very nature it relates to a transition period, during which its application was bound to diminish as the descendents of emancipated Jews became more and more absorbed into society. On the basis of his own argument he ought to have expected great Jewish composers to emerge in the future. Even so, when they in fact did emerge in the persons of Mahler and Schoenberg, his argument still illuminated something important about them. (Neither of these, incidentally, held Wagner's anti-Semitism against him: they both idolized him.) Both men were alienated from two cultures – each rejected the Jewish religion yet was a lifelong victim of anti-Semitism – and the music of both gave full expression to their personal and artistic isolation, even to its neurotic aspects.

What was happening then and since is that while with the passage of generations Jews were integrating with the Western cultural tradition, that tradition was disintegrating to meet them half way. The atomization of society, the increase in pace of change and hence problems of adjustment, the consequent rootlessness of the individual, his alienation from himself, from society, and from the past of both – these have become major themes of the culture of our time. Our age is characterized by superwars, the mass migration of entire populations, the scattering of dozens of millions of individual refugees, and by genocide. With every one of these things Jews are likely to be identified, and emotionally involved, more deeply than other people. At last they are in a position unconsciously to articulate the deepest concerns of the age they live in. The Jew has become the archetypal modern man. But this is only another way of saying that the rest of us are now almost as badly off as the Jews – which culturally speaking is true. And this is another reason for believing that we are now in the final stage before integration.

The degree of Wagner's originality in this, as in so many things, is almost bewildering. As usual he was offering explanations for what other people had not even noticed. But the trouble, again as usual, is that what was marvellous about his contribution was commingled with what was repellent to such an extent that it got overlooked and rejected along with the rest. In this case the argument I have salvaged from his anti-Semitic writings is the baby that was thrown out with the bathwater. The bathwater was foul.

Wagner's anti-Semitism is strikingly similar in its personal origins to Hitler's. The worst period of deprivation and humiliation he ever had to suffer was the two and a half years during which he tried and failed to establish himself in Paris, which was then the world capital of opera, at a time when the roost was ruled by Meyerbeer, a Jew, and the next figure to him was Halévy, also a Jew. It came close to breaking his spirit. (His fears found expression in a short story he wrote at the time about a young German composer dying in Paris in neglect, poverty and despair.) Even in its duration the period of the humiliation was roughly the same as Hitler's in the Vienna dosshouse. Both men were the sons of petty officials, both were megalomaniac, and in both of them the experience of being brought to the edge of starvation by society's total disregard of them seems to have activated a sense of persecution which bordered on paranoia, which cast "the Jews" as the villains, and which became a mad hatred that never afterwards died.

Wagner — ferociously conscious of his neglected genius, and utterly destitute — hated the works whose popular acceptance barred the way to his

own. He saw them as gimcrack and fraudulent,
which they were. In retrospect he hated them all
the more because in desperation he had succumbed
to the temptation to write like them himself.
" 'Grand Opera' stood there before me in all its
scenic and musical pomp, its emotionalism, its
striking effects, its sheer musical bulk. And the
object of my artistic ambition became not just to
copy it but to outdo it with reckless prodigality on
all fronts." So he wrote *Rienzi*, which von Bülow
once described as Meyerbeer's best opera. The
canon Wagner laid down in later life begins with
the work he wrote after that, *The Flying Dutchman.*
Rienzi has not been performed at Bayreuth to this
day.

Wagner attributed all that was meretricious in
Paris opera to the Jewishness of its composers.
"Of necessity what comes out of attempts by Jews
to make art must have the property of coldness, of
non-involvement, to the point of being trivial and
absurd. We are forced to categorize the Jewish
period in modern music as the period of con-
summate uncreativeness – stability run to seed."
Jewish music not only did but was bound to culti-
vate the surface qualities of attractiveness, technical
skill, facility, fluency, charm, glitter, surprise, the
striking effect. It was a succession of effects in the
bad sense, "effects without causes". This was why
it found its natural expression in the theatre of

unmotivated spectacle — Grand Opera. To write
works of this kind was to make use of art as a mere
means — a means of entertainment, a means of
giving pleasure and getting to be liked, a means of
achieving status, money, fame. For Jews it was a
means of making their way in an alien society.
"Like all the Parisian composers of our day Halévy
burned with enthusiasm for his art for just so long
as he needed it to help him scale the heights of
success. Once this was done and he had entered
the ranks of privileged and lionized composers he
cared nothing beyond turning out operas and
getting paid for them. In Paris fame is everything,
the artist's delight — and his destruction."

The first eight words of this quotation betray
Wagner's double standard in the very act of trying
to dissemble it. Gentile or Jew, nearly all artists
who have been famous in their day and subsequently
disregarded have been people who used their art to
please others and win social and financial success
for themselves. There is a special irony in the fact
that of all the really great composers the least
indifferent to social and financial rewards was
Wagner.

In Wagner's defence it can be said that his central
argument was correct, and decades ahead of its
time; that it illuminates many side issues; that he
acknowledged the eminence of Jewish intellectuals,
as distinct from creative artists; and that he attacked

the Christian tradition (see pp 13-14) as much as he
attacked Judaism. Against this it must be said that
although the validity of an argument is unaffected
by the motives of the person who uses it, it is still a
fact that Wagner's motives in this case were twisted;
that what is true in his argument could have been
advanced without anti-Semitism, which was therefore superfluous even from his own point of view;
and that his attacks on Christianity never had the
same personalized venom as his attacks on Judaism.

The authority which most people erroneously
suppose genius to confer has enabled Wagner's anti-
Semitism to do terrible harm. Quite apart from
anything else, Hitler made use of it. So there is
poetic justice, although neither logic nor justifica-
tion, in the fact that among the people who have
been most severely damaged by it is Wagner himself.

Three

Wagnerolatry

"We recently had a very serious conversation on the subject of Richard Wagner," Pierre Louÿs wrote to Debussy: "I merely stated that Wagner was the greatest man who had ever existed, and I went no further. I didn't say that he was God himself, though indeed I may have thought something of the sort."

The worship of Wagner by people of all kinds, including some who were themselves possessed of creative ability of the highest order, and in fields quite different from music, is something unique in the history of our culture. "Wagner's art was the great passion of Nietzsche's life," Thomas Mann has written: "He loved it as did Baudelaire, the poet of the *Fleurs du Mal*, of whom it is told that in the agony, the paralysis and the clouded mind of his last days he smiled with pleasure when he heard Wagner's name." Of himself Mann has written: "My passion for the Wagnerian enchantment has accompanied my life ever since I was first conscious of it and began to make it my own and penetrate it with my understanding. All that I owe to him, of enjoyment and instruction, I can never forget: the hours of deep and single bliss in the midst of the theatre throngs, hours of nervous and intellectual transport and rapture, perceptions of great and moving import, such as only this art vouchsafes." Commenting on this a few years later in the light of the misappropriation of Wagner by the Nazis he said: "The words express an admiration which has never been diminished, no, not even come near to being, or ever could be, by any scepticism or any unfriendly usage to which the great object of it may offer a handle." And then, later still, he described Wagner's work as "a perfectly unique eruption of talent and genius; the achievement, at once deeply serious and completely ravishing, of a magician. . . ."

One of the many extraordinary aspects of this extraordinary phenomenon is that Wagner was frequently worshipped not only in his works but in his person. King Ludwig II of Bavaria wrote to him: "I can only adore you, only praise the power that led you to me. More clearly and ever more clearly do I feel that I cannot reward you as you deserve: all I can ever do for you can be no better than stammered thanks. An earthly being cannot requite a divine spirit." If this were the only example we should write it off as a homosexual love letter but, incredibly, it was not at all uncommon for Wagner's friends to speak of him in this way. For instance

Hans von Bülow, whose wife was later to bear three illegitimate children to Wagner and then marry him, talked of "this glorious, unique man whom one must venerate like a god."

Wagner's great enemy Hanslick – the critic so spitefully caricatured as Beckmesser in *The Master-singers* – wrote in his autobiography: "He exercised an incomprehensible magic in order to make friends, and to retain them; friends who sacrificed themselves for him, and, three times offended, came three times back to him again. The more ingratitude they received from Wagner, the more zealously they thought it their duty to work for him. The hypnotic power that he everywhere exerted, not merely by his music but by his personality, overbearing all opposition and bending everyone to his will, is enough to stamp him as one of the most remarkable of phenomena, a marvel of energy and endowment."

One such friend, a man called Felix Draeseke, consoled another with these words: "At present it is not exactly agreeable to have relations with him. Later, however, in another thirty or forty years, we shall be envied by all the world, for a phenomenon like him is something so gigantic that after his death it will become ever greater and greater, particularly as then the great image of the man will no longer be disfigured by any counter-considerations."

He was right. Wagner was idolized after his death

by people of all kinds: composers as disparate as
Debussy and Mahler (who once said that in music
there was only Beethoven and Wagner "and after
them, nobody"); by people famous for their irony
and detachment, like Thomas Mann, or for their
iconoclasm, like Bernard Shaw – who once wrote
that even at performances whose incompetence beg-
gared all powers of description, even his, "most of us
are at present so helplessly under the spell of *The
Ring's* greatness that we can do nothing but go rav-
ing about the theatre between the acts in ecstasies of
deluded admiration." Wagner Societies, founded
in the composer's lifetime, flourished in many parts
of the world. The number of books and articles
written about him, which had reached the ten
thousand mark before his death, overtook those
about any other human being except Jesus and
Napoleon. The religious language that had been
used of his person continued to be used of his work:
people talked of being "converted" to his music, of
"making the pilgrimage" to Bayreuth – and were
derided by others as "fanatics". Many indeed, like
the composer Chabrier, cheerfully described themselves as fanatics.

The phenomenon has continued ever since, and
we are all familiar with it. The devotion aroused in
some people by Wagner's music is different in kind
from that aroused by any other composer's. It is like
being in love: a kind of madness, a kind of worship,

an irrational commitment yet abandonment which, among other things, dissolves the critical faculty. The best-known hatchet man in contemporary British journalism, Bernard Levin, has poured out his adoration over a whole page of the *New States-man*. After a Promenade Concert in the mid-sixties which concluded with the third act of *Götter-dämmerung* the young audience cheered for half an hour and then, when the performers finally went home and the lights of the Albert Hall were switched off, carried on cheering in the dark.

The equal and opposite reaction is just as famil-iar: the militant advocacy is equalled by a militant dislike. Wagner in his lifetime had more, and more bitter, personal enemies than any great composer has ever had, and his music can provoke a hostility not merely greater than any other but, again, dif-ferent in kind. People who would consider that to condemn the music of any other such famous com-poser as bad would be foolish if the word were meant aesthetically and meaningless if meant morally do not hesitate to apply it to Wagner's in both senses. His music is denounced, as is no other, in moral terms: it is "immoral", "corrupting", "poi-sonous", "degenerate". The notion that there is something inherently evil in it, a notion as old as the music itself, received its greatest boost from Hitler's worship of Wagner, and the composer's subsequent association with Nazism. To this day there are many

people who think there is something fascist in the
music.

Here, then, we have a music that gets at people –
not everyone, of course, but a remarkable number –
in a unique way: gets under their skins, stirs passions that no other music touches, and draws reactions which, whether favourable or unfavourable,
are essentially immoderate. "Prejudice", to quote
Grove's Dictionary of Music, "affects judgement of
Wagner more than that of almost any other composer." This fact has been notorious for a hundred
years, but it has never, so far as I know, been explained. Yet I think it can be explained.

The key is this: Wagner gives expression to
things which in the rest of us, and in the rest of art,
are unconscious because they are repressed. Modern psychology has familiarized us with the idea –
and convinced most of us of its truth – that in the
process of growing up and developing independent
personalities, and learning to live in society, we
have to subordinate some of our most powerful
instinctual desires, especially erotic and aggressive
ones – for instance passionate sexual feeling towards
parents and siblings, or the urge to attack and des-
troy those on whom we are emotionally dependent –
so that these are driven underground, below the
level of consciousness, and kept there at the cost of
some strain, as a result of which they remain charged with a high emotional voltage. Most of the

really important taboos in our society, such as the incest taboo, relate to them. This repression, this
inner conflict, is inseparable from living, and is part
of the personality of each one of us. I believe that it
is from, and to, this level of the personality that
Wagner's music speaks.

I cannot prove this, because the emotional content of music is not expressible in words, but from
what *is* expressed in words – the texts of the operas
and, quite separately, Wagner's prose writings –
evidence rises up in abundance to support it. Let us
look first at the operas. Their subject matter is, to a
remarkable degree, the subject matter of depth psychology. Even today audiences would be inexpres-
sibly shocked if the first act of a new drama were to
consist of a prolonged, passionate love scene between brother and sister which culminated in sexual
intercourse as soon as the curtain was down. Yet
this is the first act of *Die Walküre*. And in the second
act it is openly and explicitly approved. Wotan says

> *What wrong*
> *Did these two do*
> *When spring united them in love?*

And when Fricka (who, let us not forget, is the god-
dess of marriage) cries out

> *My heart shudders,*
> *My brain reels:*

> *Marital intercourse*
> *Between brother and sister!*
> *When did anyone live to see it:*
> *Brother and sister* physically *lovers?*

Wotan replies

> *You have lived to see it today.*
> *Learn from this*
> *That things can ordain themselves*
> *Though they never happened before.*
> *That these two love each other*
> *Is obvious to you.*
> *Listen to some honest advice:*
> *Smile on their love, and bless*
> *Siegmund and Sieglinde's union.*
> *Their sweet joy*
> *Will reward you for your blessing.*

And a moment later, in words which convince us, as so often, that the voice of Wagner is speaking through Wotan

> *You only want to understand,*
> *Always, what you are used to:*
> *My mind is reaching out towards*
> *Things that have never happened.*

In two of the other operas, *Siegfried* and *Parsifal*, oedipal sexuality is presented and explored. In both of them the central character is so innocent of life that he knows nothing of either sex or fear. He meets a woman whom he does not consciously identify as such. They kiss, and this awakens sexual feeling in him for the first time – and fear with it. His first thought is that this must be his mother. But she tells him that she is not – that his mother is dead and he himself is the cause. Whereupon he cries out in an agony of guilt.

As for *Tristan and Isolde*, I do not think there is a more erotic work in the whole of great art. And the salient intellectual influence on it was Schopenhauer, who anticipated Freud in so many startling ways – most importantly in his central concept of the Will, which foreshadows very closely the Freudian concept of Libido.

At one level all the mature Wagner operas except *The Mastersingers* are like animated textbooks of psychoanalysis. While archetypal psycho-sexual situations are being acted out and discussed on the stage at exhaustive length, the orchestra is pouring out a flood of the otherwise inexpressible feelings associated with them. And this is the heart of the matter: it is in the orchestra, as Wagner and everyone since has been aware, that the innermost aspects of the drama are being realized. The most important things in life, namely its psycho-emotional fundamentals *as inwardly experienced*, are articulated here, as they can never be in words, or on the stage, or in any other outward terms. The Wagnerian orchestra is, to quote Thomas Mann again, "the kingdom of subliminal knowledge, unknown to the word Up There."

Wagner knew he was making the orchestra express the world of primitive, unbridled, inchoate feeling below the level of conscious awareness. He stated the theory of it often in his prose writings. A typical example is this: "In the instruments the primal organs of creation and nature are represented. What they articulate can never be clearly determined or stipulated because they render primal feeling itself, emergent from the chaos of the first creation, when there may even have been no human beings to take it into their hearts. The particular genius of the human voice is quite different from this. It represents the human heart and all its delimitable, individual emotion. Because of this it is circumscribed in character, but also specific and clear. The thing to do now is bring the two elements together — make them one. Set the clear, specific emotion of the human heart, represented by the voice, against the wild primal feelings, with their ungovernable urge towards infinitude, represented by the instruments; it will appease and smooth the violence of those feelings and channel their cross-currents into a single, definite course. Meanwhile the human heart itself, insofar as it absorbs the primal feelings, will be infinitely enlarged and strengthened, and become capable of experiencing with godlike awareness what previously had been a mere inkling of higher things."

One might put this in Freudian language by saying that the singer's is the voice of the Ego while the orchestra is the voice of the Id, so that together they expand consciousness beyond all its normal limits into a total self-awareness which we are otherwise incapable of. Wagner knew that he was articulating what in others was repressed, and that therefore there was an abnormal wholeness about both himself and his work. "Only what is at one within itself is intelligible to feeling. What lacks internal unity, what fails to articulate itself in actual and clear form, baffles feeling and drives it over into thought – that is to say to the imposition of order – while feeling itself is suspended. The artist who addresses himself to feeling must therefore, if he is to persuade it to his ends, be already so at one within himself that he can dispense with the help of his logical apparatus and use instead, but in full consciousness, the infallible receptive powers of unconscious, pure human emotion. . . . A man who is still not at one in his own mind about what is really important to him – whose feelings are not as yet focussed on an object that will make their expression definite, indeed essential, but who, confronted with an external world of feeble, fortuitous, alien phenomena, is internally divided – such a man is incapable of this sort of expression of emotion."

One of the many things about Wagner that never
cease to astonish is the high degree to which he was
conscious of what he was doing. In his books,
abominably written though they are, he shows himself a Freudian before Freud – or perhaps rather a
Jungian before Jung, for in them he expounds with
unprecedented insight the psychic import of myth
and of dreams, and the use of symbols, and the
function of all these things as alternative languages
of unconscious feeling, and hence their unique significance for art. Even in detail, such as the extent to
which political and social institutions are illusions,
or the partial responsibility of the Christian tradition for man's alienation from his own instinctual
life, he anticipated the psychoanalysts. Eighty years
before Freud's *Civilization and Its Discontents* he expressed its central thesis in his book *Art and Revolution*. In Freud's words "it is impossible to ignore
the extent to which civilization is built up on renunciation of instinctual gratifications, the degree to
which the existence of civilization presupposes the
nongratification (suppression, repression or something else?) of powerful instinctual urgencies."
Wagner quite consciously regarded his art as being
in revolt against civilization in this sense, a re-
assertion of hitherto repressed natural feeling. In
the somewhat Marx-flavoured idiom characteristic
of his political writing at the time he expressed it as
follows: "In the progress of civilization, so inimical

to man, we can at least look forward to this happy consequence: the burdens and constraints it lays on what is natural grow to such gigantic proportions that in the end it builds up in crushed but indes- tructible nature the pressure necessary to fling them off with a single violent gesture. This whole ac- cumulation of civilization will then have served only to make nature realize its own colossal strength. But the employment of this strength is revolution. . . . It is the job of art, specifically, to reveal to this social force its own noblest import and to show it its true direction. And it is only on the shoulders of our great social movement that true art can raise itself from its present state of civilized barbarity to its rightful pre-eminence."

My central contention, then, is that Wagner's music expresses, as does no other art, repressed and highly charged contents of the psyche, and that this is the reason for its uniquely disturbing effect. To make a Freudian pun, it gets past the Censor. Some people are made to feel by it that they are in touch with the depths of their own personalities for the first time. The feeling is of a wholeness yet un- boundedness – hence, I suppose, its frequent comparison with mystical or religious experience. The passionate nature of it, its unwonted depth and its frequently erotic character also explain why it is like being in love. Most important of all, it is the abandoned utterance of what has been in some way forbidden, and thus presents us with the life of feeling which we all in our heart of hearts would like to live but which, in the real world, we can never live, a life in which our most passionate desires and their expression are unrestrained – life as it would be if the Id could have its way. This is what is so spellbinding about it: it fulfils in art our most heartfelt wishes, which can never be fulfilled in life. This is why it seems to transcend – and to expand the consciousness of its listeners beyond – the bounds of what is possible; why it is so commonly spoken of as a form of wizardry or hypnosis; why even such a writer as Mann is moved to use words like "magic", "enchantment" and the rest.

Wagner the man possessed some of the qualities of his music to an extraordinary degree. For instance his life was characterized by the same profound eroticism. His greatest biographer, Ernest Newman, wrote at one point in *Wagner as Man and Artist*: "I have given the erotic history of Wagner in such detail not only because of the enormous part the erotic played in his life and in the shaping of his character, but because to know him thoroughly from this side is to have the key to his whole nature." He was whole in the sense that his music is whole: what is elsewhere repressed was in him lived. Röckel, describing the rehearsals for the first performance of *Tristan*, says: "He would listen with closed eyes to the artists singing to Bülow's pianoforte accompaniment. If a difficult passage went particularly well he would spring up, embrace or kiss the singer warmly, or out of pure joy stand on his head on the sofa, creep under the piano, jump up on to it, run into the garden and scramble joyously up a tree. . . ." Liszt, describing a meeting with Wagner, wrote: "When he saw me he wept, laughed and ranted for joy for at least a quarter of an hour." References to him of this kind are numberless. Of the general portraits we have of him the following, from Edouard Schuré, is typical: "When he showed himself he broke out as a whole like a torrent bursting its dikes. One stood dazzled before that exuberant and protean nature, ardent, personal, excessive in everything, yet marvellously equilibrated by the predominance of a devouring intellect. The frankness and extreme audacity with which he showed his nature, the qualities and defects of which were exhibited without concealment, acted on some people like a charm, while others were repelled by it."

We can see why the man's personality affected so many of the people who knew him in the same way as his music affects so many listeners. Some were overwhelmed, and worshipped. Others regarded his almost incredible lack of restraint as shocking or frightening, or mad, or immoral, or in some other way deeply disturbing. Some felt it as a threat to their own personalities, and recoiled, and denounced. Similarly in the music, the same qualities repel as attract: the sensationalism, the eroticism, the sweeping away of inhibition, the enactment of what is taboo. Being put in touch with their own depths may be a uniquely rich and satisfying experience for some people but others are revolted. To these Wagner's music is the voice of the prohibited: it speaks out their forbidden selves. So they denounce it in moral terms – "dangerous", "disgusting", "vulgar", "excessive", "self-indulgent", "sick".

Sometimes it is the people who come most deeply under the spell who then get most frightened and react most violently. Nietzsche, the supreme Wagnerolater, became the supreme Wagnerphobe. In his last book, *Nietzsche Contra Wagner,* he wrote: "Apparently you think *all* music . . . must leap out of the wall and shake the listener to his very intestines. Only then do you consider music 'effective'. But on *whom* are such effects achieved? On those whom a noble artist should never impress: on the mass, on the immature, on the blasé, on the sick, on the idiots, on *Wagnerians*!" And again: "*Parsifal* is a work of perfidy, of vindictiveness, of a secret attempt to poison the presuppositions of life – a *bad* work. . . . I despise everyone who does not experience *Parsifal* as an attempted assassination of basic ethics." In his biography of Debussy, Edward

Lockspeiser has written: "It is certain that Debussy's attitude to Wagner was complex, compounded of love and fear, displaying many contradictions and compelling him to lash out with ironic jibes at the object of his admiration." And another composer, Chausson, once wrote: "The red spectre of Wagner . . . does not let go of me. I reach the point of detesting him. Then I look through his pages, trying to find hidden vices in him, and I find them."

Such fascinated detestation is a kind of inverse love. It is revealing that among Nietzsche's last words on the subject were: "I suppose I know better than anyone the prodigious feats of which Wagner was capable, the fifty worlds of strange ecstasies to which no one else had wings to soar; and as I am alive today and strong enough to turn even the most suspicious and most dangerous things to my own advantage, and thus to grow stronger, I declare Wagner to have been the greatest benefactor of my life."

If my analysis of the Wagner magic is correct it explains why his work seems to have a special appeal for the emotionally isolated or repressed: Proust, living alone in his cork-lined room; Wittgenstein, who was almost as solitary as Nietzsche; Albert Schweitzer, who turned his back on the Western world to live out his life in the African jungle; Bernard Shaw, undersexed and unable to relate to others except through ideas. And this is not to mention the composers, for instance Richard Strauss – of whom Lotte Lehmann, who revered him, has written: "As a rule he appeared utterly aloof and impersonal, so cold in his reaction to people that they would withdraw instantly and give up any misguided attempt at friendliness"; Mahler and Schoenberg, both of them neurotic and alienated to a degree; the celibate Bruckner. I am not, of course, saying that Wagner appeals to all emotionally deprived people, or only to deprived people; but the words of Mann which I quoted earlier about "deep and single bliss in the midst of the theatre throngs" touch on something crucial about this art's power: it makes possible a passionate warmth and fullness of emotion without personal relationships.

Not only does the music seem to have a particular appeal to the isolated and the odd: there is actually a longstanding belief that some people are unhinged by it. As long ago as 1891 *The Musical Times* quoted *The Boston Home Journal* as saying: "Marie Wilt, the soprano who lately committed suicide, once learned the part of Brünnhilde in three weeks. 'That finished me', she said shortly before her death. Schnorr died shortly after *Tannhäuser*.* Anders went mad studying *Tristan*, and Scaria after *Parsifal* died insane." Before this is dismissed as utter nonsense let it be

*This is a mistake — it was *Tristan*.

remembered that Wagner himself feared that something of the sort might be true. He once began a letter to Mathilde Wesendonk with the words:

"Child! This *Tristan* is turning into something *fearful*!

"That last act!!! –

"I'm afraid the opera will be forbidden – unless the whole thing is turned into a parody by bad production –: only mediocre performances can save me! Completely *good* ones are bound to drive people mad, – I can't imagine what else could happen...."

When Ludwig Schnorr von Carolsfeld, the tenor who sang the first Tristan, died almost immediately afterwards in a delirium of Wagner-worship, the composer felt his work to be responsible. He continued to believe that only strong characters could immerse themselves in it with impunity. He would certainly have agreed that those who despise, deride or denounce his music are protecting themselves from a real, not an imagined, danger.

People who regard this music as, in a unique way, evil, can use solid arguments to support themselves. First, it is simply true that it speaks with almost overpowering eloquence of incest wishes and unrestrained eroticism, of hatred and malice, spite, anxiety, guilt, isolation, foreboding, concealed menace, the whole dark side of life. Second, there really is serious reason to believe that this may imperil the stability of some people. Third, it is – in the sense discussed earlier – hostile to civilization. This last point constitutes the truthful element in the belief that there is something fascist about it – this and the unbridled violence with which destructive passions are expressed.

The Wagnerian would reply, first, that all these frightening passions are a part of life, and a most important part too, whether in the big world outside or in the privacies of the individual psyche. Without them no depiction of reality is complete, or even adequate, and any that purports to be is evasive. (This is one of the reasons for *The Ring*'s uniqueness as an attempt to depict the whole of reality in a single work of art.) Second, they form only part of the content of Wagner's music and not the whole, just as they form part of reality and not the whole. One of the operas, *The Mastersingers*, is all summer, warm and overflowing with human affection and the love of life and art. And some of the best-known music in the others depicts the natural world – the Forest Murmurs, the Fire Music and so on. Some of it is so pictorial and two-dimensional that one might almost call it poster music. One of the many unique things about Wagner's music, in fact, is the completeness of its range along the inner-reality/ outer-reality axis. Third, this music does for some people what psychoanalysis claims to do for others: it releases radioactive material from the depths of the personality and confronts them with it and makes them feel it and live it through. It also relates all this inner feeling harmoniously to an outer reality. It can thus help to put people at one with both their inner selves and the external world; so in a sense it is the most whole-making, the most therapeutic art. Fourth, it is anti-civilized only in the sense in which civilization is the enemy of natural feeling and hence the cause of neurosis. This and the previous point mean that not only is it not "sick", it is unusually healthy. As for the charge that it is fascist, this is mere guilt by association, Wagner's works have nothing whatever to do with blond Ayrans, jackboots or the gassing of Jews, and to suppose that they have is to accept the perversion of them propagated by the Nazis. The implications of *The Ring* are the precise opposite of fascism: that the pursuit of power is incompatible with a life of true feeling, and therefore the attainment of it destroys the capacity for love; and that because power is inwardly destructive of the people who wield it, it is in the very deepest sense anti-life; that necessary order should rest not on force but on consent and the honouring of agreements; and therefore that the dishonouring of agreements, because it ensures that things can be settled only by force, and therefore will be settled by force, is the most disruptive of crimes.

To some music-lovers, Wagner is simply a composer like any other, and to these Wagner-

olatry and Wagnerphobia are alike enigmatic. But
for the rest of us there is much more to it than that.
For us there is something uniquely ambiguous about
this music. However beautiful it may be – and many
people, including some of the greatest composers
since Wagner, have thought it as beautiful as any
that has ever been written – it is never only an end in
itself, always also a carrier of something else; and it
is how we react to the something else that is decisive.
To some this music is like the poisoned flowers of
the Borgias; to others like requited love. There is no
medium in which such differences can be settled, for
the realm in which they lie is not merely deeper than
words, it is deeper than music.

Four

The Influence of Wagner

THE most influential poem of our century in any language, *The Waste Land,* contains four quotations from Wagner's operas (two from *Tristan and Isolde* and two from *Götterdämmerung*) and a line from Verlaine's sonnet on Wagner's *Parsifal.* In addition, part of the central section of the poem parallels the first scene of the third act of *Götterdämmerung*, with Thames-daughters substituted for Rhine-daughters. What may well be the most influential of modern novels, those of Joyce, are pervaded with Wagnerian reference. When, in *Ulysses,* Stephen Dedalus cries "*Nothung*!" as he lifts his ashplant to smash a chandelier in a Dublin brothel we are given not just the cry itself from *The Ring* but a reminder of the fact that the tree in which Nothung had been embedded by Wotan was an ash, and that Wotan's spear, the chief power symbol in *The Ring*, was an ashplant. In the same novel we have the chanting of the blood-brotherhood oath from *Götterdämmerung*. In *Finnegans Wake* we have the extensive parallels with *Tristan,* plus a personal reference to Wagner – the "wagoner" and his "mudheeldy wheesindonk" is Wagner ("Wagner" means "wagoner" in German) and Mathilde Wesendonk, with whom he was having an affair at the time when he composed *Tristan*.

On all these works the influence of Wagner extends beyond direct quotation, and beyond imagery, to the structure itself, for in them his technique of weaving a seamless fabric out of fragmentary leitmotifs is consciously adapted from music to literature. Most important of all, the use of the interior monologue in the novel originated as an attempt to make words do in fiction what Wagner's orchestra had done in his operas. The novelist who introduced it, Edouard Dujardin (whose *Les Lauriers Sont Coupés*, according to the *Oxford Companion to French Literature*, "is said to have given James Joyce the idea for the form of Ulysses"), was founder and editor of the *Revue Wagnerienne*, which existed from 1885 to 1888 – while he was also writing the novel, which was published in 1888.

These examples alone are enough to show that Wagner's influence on modern literature is of major importance. It is wide as well as deep – in one way or another it crops up in the work of most of the outstanding writers since his time. When we remember that during the same period he was the greatest single influence on music and opera, and perhaps on the theatre – and that his influence has been important on a number of leading philosophers, politicians and even painters – we find ourselves confronted with a *range* of influence on the part of one man for which there is no recent parallel.

The extent to which this has been ignored in our day is almost incredible. The only explanation I can think of is that Wagner went through a period of such deep unpopularity in the generation before our own that its members were simply not inclined to consider him as an influence on the artists they admired. For instance *The Waste Land* must be the most written-about poem of this century, but I do not remember coming across any extensive discussion of the Wagnerian elements in it. W. H. Auden has esteemed Eliot all his life, and presumably knows *The Waste Land* as well as anyone – and he loves opera – but in his most recent volume of essays he tells how it was only a reading of Nietzsche's *The Wagner Case* "which first taught me to listen to Wagner, about whom I had previously held silly preconceived notions." Anyone who writes about Wagner is forcibly made aware how widespread these notions are. And prejudice can survive any amount of evidence.

But the time has come to confront the Wagner phenomenon; to acknowledge, and critically evaluate, his influence on the culture of our age. To do this properly would itself require a book, and one I am not equipped to write. In fact I am not competent to go deeply into the work of even one of the artists concerned, let alone all of them. What I want to do in this chapter is sketch the *extent* of what needs to be considered – mark out a surface area on the ground into which, I hope, others will dig.

The first cultural centre to come under Wagnerian domination was Paris in the late 1880s. "Writers not only discussed musical subjects, but judged painting, literature, and philosophy from a Wagnerian point of view", Romain Rolland tells us: "The whole universe was seen and judged in the thought of Bayreuth." And of the years immediately after, Léon Daudet wrote: "We studied his characters as if Wotan held the secret of the world and Hans Sachs were the spokesman for free, natural and spontaneous art." This situation had been building up long before the 1880s. As far back as the 1850s French poets had been writing enthusiastically in the Paris press about Wagner productions they had seen in Germany – Gerard de Nerval about the première of *Lohengrin* in 1850, Gautier about *Tannhäuser* in 1857. The Wagner concerts in Paris in 1860 swept Baudelaire off his feet and made Wagner his ruling passion. The essay he wrote on *Richard Wagner et Tannhäuser* was to provide the Symbolists with their favourite quotations about the interdependence of the arts. (The two greatest French poets of two successive generations each wrote only one essay on a composer, and in each case it was Wagner – after Baudelaire came Mallarmé with *Richard Wagner, Rêverie d'un Poète Français*.) The sixties saw the beginnings of Wagnerolatry – first with Baudelaire, then with Villiers and the Gautiers. Théopile Gautier's daughter Judith, who was later to have an affair with Wagner, wrote of those days: "What this wonderful genius meant to us it would have been difficult even to make clear to those who were not of us – at that time when only a little group of disciples stood by the Master, sticking up for him against the jeers of the masses who failed to comprehend him. . . . We had the fanaticism of priests and martyrs, even for the slaying of our adversaries! It would, in fact, have been impossible to convince us that we should not be entirely justified in annihilating all those scoffers blind to the new radiance which was so clear to us."

Wagner was – both directly and, through Baudelaire, indirectly – the acknowledged progenitor of the Symbolist movement. Their work is pervaded with references to him, many of them idolatrous. What influenced them most was not his operas but his prose writings, in which he expounded a new theory of the relationship of the arts to each other, and particularly of poetry to music. But the operas did have their importance. Verlaine's sonnet on *Parsifal* has already been mentioned. References to *Lohengrin* are ubiquitous in the poetry of Laforgue (who was to have such a profound influence on Eliot). And we have this description of the leader of the movement at the Sunday Wagner concerts: "Sitting there among the other listeners, bent over in an attitude of meditation and concentration, the music made him seem far away; and slowly he took out a pencil from his pocket and solemnly began to write, on a worthless scrap of paper which he hid from sight with elegant modesty. The orchestra dictated and Mallarmé wrote."

It was not only Symbolist writers, nor for that matter Parisians, who were enthusiastic Wagnerians. There was a Wagner Society in Marseilles, one of whose members was Zola – who wrote in a letter: "What you call repetitions occur in all my books. This is a literary device that I began by using with some timidity, but have since pushed perhaps to excess. In my view it gives more body to a work, and strengthens its unity. The device is somewhat akin to the motifs of Wagner, and if you will ask some musical friends of yours to explain his use of these, you will understand pretty well my use of the device in literature." Wagner continued to be a major influence on French writers of all kinds; and in after years extensive references to him were to appear in the work not only of the literary heirs of the Symbolists, like Valéry and Proust, but in writers as different from these as Colette.

Another member of the Marseilles Wagner

Society at the same time as Zola was Cézanne, one of whose pictures was called *Overture to Tannhäuser*. Renoir, at his own request, painted a portrait of Wagner, having journeyed from Naples to Sicily in the hope ,of being allowed to do so. In fact it was in the conversations between these two in Palermo in 1882 that "Impressionism" was first used as a term applied to music. Gauguin, about to put France and, come to that, Western civilization behind him for ever, wrote to a friend just before he left for Tahiti: "I haven't said goodbye to the artists who think as I do. It is enough for me to remember this statement of Wagner. . . ." At a lower level of exaltation, Fantin Latour and Redon both, like Aubrey Beardsley in England, produced series of lithographs of scenes from the Wagner operas. Both Degas and Whistler were labelled Wagnerian by their contemporaries. Gustave Doré was one of Wagner's personal friends.

But his biggest influence was, not unnaturally, in the sphere of music. Debussy was so strongly under this influence while writing *Pélleas et Mélisande* that he said in a letter to another Wagner-drunk composer, Chausson, that he kept having to tear up pages of the score because "the ghost of old Klingsor* . . . would appear at the turning of

* The name of Klingsor, the evil magician in *Parsifal*, has often been used as a nickname for Wagner. It was also used by the gifted French poet who published under the name Tristan Klingsor, and wrote, among other things, the poems set by Ravel in *Shéhérazade*.

one of the bars." Both Saint-Saëns and Gounod
had become friends of Wagner in the 1860s, and
both were to remain permanently and obviously
under his musical influence. (After the disastrous
reception of *Tannhäuser* in Paris in 1861 Gounod
exclaimed: "I wish God would grant it to me to
write a flop like that!") Bizet said of Wagner: "The
charm of his music is unutterable, inexpressible. It
is voluptuousness, tenderness, love." At one performance of *Tristan* at Bayreuth in 1889 Chabrier
burst into tears, and Lekeu fainted and had to be
carried out. César Franck's music was obviously
Wagnerian. And Massenet was nicknamed "Made-
moiselle Wagner".

And all this was just in France. In the German-
speaking world the first man of genius to come
under the Wagner spell was Nietzsche, in the 1870s.
In the words of his English biographer and trans-
lator, R. J. Hollingdale, Wagner was "the most
powerful and enduring influence upon him – an
influence which, despite all his efforts, Nietzsche
could not shake off until his dying day. . . . Nietzsche
regarded his association with Wagner as the greatest
event of his life." His first book, *The Birth of Tragedy*,
is dedicated to Wagner and culminates in a hymn
of praise to him; his last, *Nietzsche Contra Wagner*,
is an anthology of his invective against the composer; and in almost every book between, Wagner
is a major presence. Since Nietzsche himself has

had an extraordinary influence – on such philosophers as Jaspers, Heidegger and Sartre, on such poets as Rilke and George, on Thomas Mann, on Bernard Shaw – this also raises the question of what might be called secondary Wagner infection.

Mann and Shaw, as I showed in the last chapter, were Wagnerites on their own account. In his book *Thomas Mann* J. M. Lindsay writes: "It is almost impossible to overstate Mann's feeling of kinship with Wagner." For all his ironic detachment he rhapsodized about Wagner's operas all his life in a Nietzschean way. A typical example is: "Marvels, *Wunderwerke* . . . no description better fits these amazing manifestations of art; and to nothing else in the whole history of artistic production are they more applicable – certain of the greatest achievements of architecture, a few Gothic cathedrals, alone excepted. . . ." One of his long stories, about the death of a creative artist, is called *Death in Venice* (Wagner died in Venice) though the personality of the central character is moulded on the Wagnerolater Mahler. Another of the stories is called *Tristan*. But more even than with Eliot or Joyce, or Zola, the influence of Wagner goes through to the structure itself. Mann specifically thought of his novels as being constructed like Wagner's operas, and as using Wagner's methods. The form of his most ambitious work, *Joseph*, is

that of *The Ring* not only in that it is a tetralogy, but
also in that it raises to its highest level the use of
leitmotifs in the novel.

Shaw, too, thought of his most ambitious work,
Back To Methuselah, as his *Ring.* In addition he also
wrote a book about *The Ring,* called *The Perfect
Wagnerite.* But like the Symbolists he was affected
most deeply by Wagner's theoretical writings. It
was Wagner who had shown, he thought, how a
theatre audience's interest and concentration on a
sustained exposition of ideas could be maintained
by infusing the ideas with passion – what Wagner,
we may remember, had called "the emotionalizing
of the intellect" – and he regarded himself as
adapting this to prose drama.

Shaw, though a pioneer of Wagnerism in England,
was no lone prophet. Bulwer Lytton had written
poetry about *Tannhäuser* well back in the composer's
lifetime. Swinburne wrote poems about *Lohengrin,
Tristan and Isolde* and *The Death of Richard Wagner.*
There are references to Wagner throughout the
novels of George Moore and Charles Morgan, and
some quite important ones in Oscar Wilde – Dorian
Gray used to sit "listening in rapt pleasure to
Tannhäuser, and seeing in the prelude to that great
work of art a presentation of the tragedy of his own
soul." An even more famous fictional character,
Sherlock Holmes, was a Wagnerite. But it was with
Shaw first, then Joyce and Eliot, that Wagnerism

became structural in the work of major writers. Books by novelists as diverse as Ford Maddox Ford, Arnold Bennett, Virginia Woolf, E. M. Forster and Willa Cather contain Wagnerism as a vital ingredient. D. H. Lawrence wrote a whole Wagnerian novel: *The Trespasser,* published in 1912. Its original title was *The Saga of Siegmund.* The heroine, Helena, is learning German because she wants "to understand Wagner in his own language". She and the hero, Siegmund, whistle and endlessly discuss bits of Wagner's music. Everything is assimilated by them into a pseudo-Wagnerian world – the Isle of Wight is "Sieglinde's island", the barking of sheep-dogs reminds them of Fafner and Fasolt, the sound of a foghorn is "the call of the horn across the sea to Tristan" and so on. It is unbelievably awful, but Wagner must have had an enormous impact on Lawrence to make him write it. In fact Richard Aldington, in his book about Lawrence, finds "the essence of Lawrence's beliefs and teachings" in Wagner's *The Work of Art of the Future.*

As for music itself, there is little that need be said. Liszt, though Wagner's father-in-law, was only a couple of years older than him, and their mutual influence in music is almost impossible to disentangle from the intertwining of their lives. Dvořák "came under the spell of Wagner", writes Julius Harrison, "and it took him some years to expunge this influence from his own compositions".

Bruckner was a naive hero-worshipper. Tchaikovsky acknowledged Wagner's influence, and was
himself the most influential of Russian composers.
The list could go on. I have already quoted from
the letter in which Mahler wrote to his wife, only
seven years before his death, that in music there
was only Beethoven "and Richard – and after them,
nobody." (Mahler in his turn has been the greatest
single influence on such outstanding composers
since as Shostakovich and Britten.) The young
Richard Strauss was nicknamed "Richard the
Second". Elgar loved only one opera, *Parsifal*, and
his masterpiece, *The Dream of Gerontius*, is in every
bar the work of a man who loved *Parsifal*. Schoenberg by the age of twenty-five had seen Wagner's
operas between twenty and thirty times each, and
the music he wrote at that time was Wagner-
sodden. (Long afterwards some of the most beautiful music of his pupils was still, in spite of the
revolution they had made, thoroughgoingly Wagnerian – for instance some of the songs of Alban
Berg. And of course another of his pupils, Webern,
was the fountain-head of the new music after the
Second World War.) The young Debussy, the
young Delius, the young Holst, the young Bartok –
Wagnerians all. There is only one major figure in
music since Wagner who seems never to have come
under his influence and that is Stravinsky. And he
has told us how his teacher Rimsky-Korsakov,

whom he never ceased to revere, "kept a portrait of Wagner over his desk".

The ground covered by this chapter is still incomplete. I have said nothing of the revolution in stage lighting inaugurated by Adolphe Appia in his designs for Wagner production and now part of the standard technique of Western theatre. I have not attempted to deal with living artists, whose own lasting merit is unpredictable; but W. H. Auden, who is widely regarded as the foremost living poet in the English-speaking world, has described Wagner as "perhaps the greatest genius that ever lived". In any case I have mentioned only English, French and German literature. What of all the rest? Are there more Italian writers like D'Annunzio, that lifelong Wagnerian who wrote, like Lawrence, an entirely Wagnerian novel? And are there Lawrences and D'Annunzios in yet other languages? I do not know. And how does one assess the influence of Wagner on the life and work of Wagnerians who were not creative artists, but who may be as important in other fields, and as different, as Hitler and Schweitzer? Again I do not know. But the very incompleteness of what I have written can only mean that the extent of Wagner's influence is greater than I have specified.

Hitler was fond of saying: "Whoever wants to understand National Socialist Germany must know

Wagner." And although the Nazi representation of Wagner, as of Nietzsche, was a perversion – indeed an *in*version as regards fundamentals – it happened, it is part of history, and it must be included in any consideration of the effect Wagner has had on our time. At the opposite end of the political spectrum Raymond Williams, writing in *The Guardian* in 1966, speaks of "a particular North Atlantic definition and structure of 'the modern'. . . . A tradition already. . . ." He is highly critical of this tradition, which he characterizes as "post-liberalism". It rests, in his view, on certain key books, of which he names eight. Half of these are in some significant sense Wagnerian: Nietzsche's *The Birth of Tragedy* and *The Genealogy of Morals*, Freud's *Civilization and its Discontents* and Thomas Mann's *Death in Venice*. So it would appear that whoever wants to understand post-liberalism must know Wagner too.

The great misfortune of Wagner's reputation is that he has been blamed for things he was not responsible for – and, in consequence, denied credit which is his due. Many things in modern life which we take for granted were originated by him. I am not thinking only of such things as international music festivals, which impinge on comparatively few people, but of more everyday matters. "We owe it to Wagner," writes Edward J. Dent in his book *Opera*, "that the auditorium is darkened as a matter of course during a performance, that the doors are shut and latecomers made to wait outside; we owe it to him that a soft prelude is heard in silence, and applause reserved for the end of an act." In another part of the same book he writes: "Wagner invented the steam curtain; steam was released from a row of jets along the line of the footlights, which gave it whatever colour was desired. . . . Another Wagnerian innovation was the use of scenery that moved sideways. . . . It is entirely to Wagner's initiative that we owe the modern developments of stage machinery." And elsewhere: "It was he who started the outlook on orchestral music which has led to the modern idolisation of the star conductor." Conductors themselves would agree on this last point, and indeed go further. Sir John Barbirolli has written: "As prime inspirer and founder of the modern school of conducting, I think we can safely point to Wagner; and a survey of his chief disciples, such as Bülow, Richter, Levi, and Mottl, quickly brings us to our own times."

I cannot begin to claim, then, that I have dealt with all aspects of Wagner's influence, or even named all the major artists who have come under that influence. But I take it no one is going to maintain that there have been many others since his time who are *more* important than those I have mentioned – many novelists more important than Proust, Joyce, Lawrence and Mann; many poets better than Baudelaire and Eliot; many more influential moral-

ists and critics than Nietzsche and Shaw; many
better composers than Bruckner, Tchaikovsky,
Dvořák, Debussy, Mahler, Strauss, Elgar and
Schoenberg. And if no more than this is agreed it
means that Wagner has had a greater influence than
any other single artist on the culture of our age.

Five

Wagner in Performance

"GREAT MUSIC," said Schnabel, "is music that's better than it can be played." A simple but eloquent demonstration of this can be got by comparing the Brahms symphonies as conducted by Toscanini and Bruno Walter. Under Toscanini they are played with an almost demonic ferocity and drive, and are deeply disturbing. Under Walter they have a glowing, autumnal relaxation and warmth, and are deeply consoling. Neither conductor transgresses the letter of the scores, nor their spirit. Yet the sum of what they bring out in them could not possibly be combined in a single performance. The acidity and cutting edge of the one entirely precludes the loving embrace of the other. High tension and heartsease are mutually exclusive. Everything each gives us is unquestionably there in the music, but for every element that is realized in performance some other has had to be sacrificed.

All this is true of the other performing arts too. A great play is one that's better than it can be performed, and so is a great opera (though possibly only the operas of Mozart and Wagner are great in this sense).

It means we can get to know great works only by incompatible performances, each of which defines the need for the others. Even the creative artist performing his own work cannot transcend this limitation, so not even his own performances can be "definitive". No doubt this is why great composers have given such widely differing performances of their own works. But since we *need* different sorts of performance we should always be open to new approaches to (or perhaps from) great works of art. Our view of them should never become fixed. If any one way of performing an artist's work becomes traditional it impoverishes our conception of it. Or rather, traditions of performance have a value, but they do serious damage if they are allowed to be exclusive.

So the first thing to say about Wagner in performance is that there is no right way, and no one way is enough. So I am not going to put forward a coherent theory of how it should be done. A producer or conductor or designer must have a unified view of any work he is engaged on while he is engaged on it, but he may do it in different ways at different times in his life with equal success.

However, there are problems of performance which are peculiar to Wagner, and I want to discuss some of these. The fact that he worked in a composite art form in which the different elements are more or less successfully fused makes this difficult, because one cannot discuss the elements all at once, yet to consider them separately is to assume a radically false view. However, if we are to talk about them at all we have to start somewhere; and as the original creative germ of Wagner's works was always musical the best starting point is probably the music.

The acts of Wagner's operas – which are, so to speak, the constructive units of his work – are the longest uninterrupted stretches of great music in existence. From curtain-up on *Götterdämmerung* to the end of Act I is about two hours. Act III of *The Mastersingers* is longer. And of course most of the works consist of three acts. One of them consists of four operas. It is a scale that has no parallel elsewhere in music, least of all in the symphonic literature, and it makes the works exceedingly difficult to sustain in performance. Only too easily can they sag and become boring. Seeing to it that they do not makes huge demands on the conductor. The first thing it requires of him is a quite abnormal mastery of architectonics. Not only must he have an assured grasp of these enormous wholes – the whole of each work and the whole of each act – he must also have a command of detail that can relate it to those wholes without sacrificing anything of it – that can show it as interesting, expressive, beautiful in itself and at the same time a functioning part of the architecture. When this happens the whole is kept before us in

every moment while the music seems to unfold with
inevitable rightness. The great Wagner conductor is
like the builder of bridges who makes a single soar-
ing arc out of three huge spans over an ebb and flow
which has a life of its own down to the last glancing
fleck of spray. Because of this unique range of demands it has always been the greatest Wagner conductors who were the greatest conductors – Richter,
Mahler, Toscanini, Furtwängler, Bruno Walter, to
name only the dead – though they were not always
the best conductors of Bach, or Mozart, or even
Beethoven. Many conductors whose performances
of some other composer's work are unsurpassed fall
short when it comes to Wagner because his organic
unities elude them. The best they can give us is one
beautiful episode after another.

It is astounding just how different these works can
be under different conductors. An objective indica-
tion of this is provided by differences in timings. At
Bayreuth, where they have complete records, the
slowest *Parsifal* to date was conducted in 1931 by
Toscanini (usually thought of as a fast conductor)
and lasted 4 hours and 48 minutes excluding intervals.
The quickest was conducted by Clemens Krauss in
1953 and lasted 3 hours 44 minutes. These differences break down as follows: under Toscanini the prelude lasted 17 minutes, under Krauss 12; with Act I
under Toscanini, 2 hours 6 minutes, under Krauss
1 hour 39 minutes; Act II under Toscanini, 1 hour

12 minutes, under Krauss 56 minutes; Act III under Toscanini, 1 hour 30 minutes, under Krauss 1 hour 9 minutes. And although these timings are extreme they are not eccentric; the other conductors of the work range the whole gamut between them. And so it is with all the operas. Even the one-act *Rheingold* reveals differences of up to half an hour: the fastest, under Suitner, is 2 hours 14 minutes, the slowest, under Knappertsbusch, 2 hours 42 minutes. Often the figures show the facts to be contrary to a conductor's reputation – Toscanini's *Tristan*, like his *Parsifal*, was the slowest ever. Often they show that the impression of a performance which has been formed by the listener is illusory – when I heard the broadcast of Karajan's *Tristan* from Bayreuth in 1952 I thought it was one of the slowest pieces of great conducting I had ever heard, but the figures show him to have taken it faster than all but one other conductor before or since.

In all music the impression we get of tempo has little to do with the mathematical measurement of time and much to do with the inner life of the performance. Beecham was always thought of as a conductor who sent things along at a pretty fast lick, but a comparison of the stop-watch timings of his performances with those of other conductors shows this not to be literally so. The impression was made by an uncommon buoyancy and spring at speeds which were fairly average. When he conducted *The*

Mastersingers at Covent Garden for the first time in
1913 he was criticized for taking it so much faster
than Richter (who had not just studied the work
with Wagner but lived with him during its composition and helped him copy out the score) whereupon
he produced timings to prove that his performance
was *slower* than Richter's. Wagner learned this
truth the hard way. He furnished his early scores
with what he later called "positively eloquent indications of tempo, fixing these with unmistakable
precision (so I thought) by means of the metronome.
But then whenever I heard about some foolishly
wrong tempo in, say, a performance of my *Tannhäuser*, any complaint from me was always met with
the defence that my metronome markings had been
most scrupulously observed. From this I realized
how uncertain the relationship of mathematics to
music must be, and not only dispensed with the
metronome forthwith but contented myself with
only the most general indications of even the main
tempo...." He came to feel that what more than
anything else gives life to a good performance is not
even this main tempo but innumerable tiny *modi-
fications* of tempo that could not possibly be indica-
ted by words or figures, but must flow intuitively
from the performer. Finding the right tempo in this
musical and not mathematical sense of something
almost quiveringly alive seemed to him the key to
the whole art of conducting: if this was wrong, noth-

ing else could go really right, whereas if this was right the other aspects of performance would tend naturally to fall into place. It came, he believed, from an instinctive feel for the *melos*, the singing inner voice that is at the heart of all music. And his attitude became one of "if you can't *feel* what the tempo ought to be, and how it ought to change, it's no good my trying to tell you."

His own performances of his music were very much on the fast side. I once timed all the available recordings of the prelude to *The Mastersingers*: the longest lasted ten and a half minutes and the shortest eight and three quarters; yet when Wagner himself conducted it in Mannheim in 1871 it lasted only "a few seconds more than eight minutes." On one occasion we find him complaining of a performance of the overture to *Tannhäuser* that it had lasted twenty minutes, pointing out that under his own baton in Dresden it had lasted twelve. He also complained of a performance of *Rheingold* in Augsburg that it had taken three hours, and reminded everyone that under a conductor coached by himself it had lasted two and a half. Levi, who conducted the first *Parsifal* under Wagner's close personal supervision, took the work faster than all but four of the conductors at Bayreuth during the ninety-five years since. Liszt, after conducting the première of *Lohengrin* at Weimar in 1850, received a letter of complaint from Wagner that the performance had taken a full hour too long.

The noisy, ponderous performances with which we are still familiar and which seem by now to have shaped the popular view of Wagner were opposed to his wishes and to his practice, and were a cause of lifelong complaint from him. When he built his own opera house he designed the whole building round the orchestra pit, putting it in a place that made noisiness impossible. "The first essential I felt was that the vast musical machine, namely the orchestra, should be hidden. This primary consideration necessitated a complete rearrangement of the auditorium. . . ." He not only buried the orchestra under the stage but went on to surround the necessary opening with his famous *Schalldeckel*, a black (and therefore, in the darkness, invisible) curved wooden shield that throws the sound *away* from the audience. The singers confront the audience direct, without any intervening orchestra pit, and their voices fill the auditorium with ease and presence over soft orchestral sound from an unidentifiable source, warm and diffused in quality, every sharp edge removed. The result is very beautiful and quite unlike anywhere else. Bayreuth is frequently said to have the best acoustics in the world. But Rudolf Kempe once complained to me – and no one could call him a noisy conductor – that there are some scenes in which it is simply not possible to get enough volume out into the auditorium: the Ride of the Valkyries, for instance, and Siegfried's Funeral March. When Furtwängler was conducting at Bayreuth in the 1930s he tried to get the *Schalldeckel* removed, but was foiled in the attempt. Richard Strauss, another Bayreuth conductor, expressed a preference for the open pit of the Italian theatre.

Admittedly there is a bloom, a bite, some quality of sensory immediacy missing from the orchestral sound at Bayreuth, and sometimes the singers blur the orchestral detail. But I think the advantages more than compensate for this. For me the question is settled in favour of Bayreuth by its *dramatic* advantages. The visible presence of musicians between us and the stage (the conductor if we are sitting in the stalls, the entire orchestra of a hundred or more if we are in a raised part of the house) tugging at our awareness with their reading lights and ceaseless physical movements, provides us with a human scale against which we cannot help seeing the singers. In Bayreuth there is nothing but the stage to impinge even subliminally on the eye, and by means of positioning, lighting and adroit use of sets the singers can be made to appear almost any size – a particular asset when the characters of the drama are dwarfs, giants and gods. Another thing is that in the Italian type of house it is psychologically impossible not to relate the sound of the orchestra to its visible presence there in front of you, and thus to *locate* its sound. It rises up before you like a transparent plane, a plate-glass window between you and the singers which their voices have to penetrate to reach you. In Bayreuth, where the auditorium is plunged into blackness and the orchestral sound begins all around you in the dark, it seems to exist equally in every part of the theatre, and this illusion is maintained after the curtain goes up, not only because there is still no locatable source but also because you are immediately up against the voices. Instead of being like a screen dividing singers and audience it is a common element in which both are, surrounding and uniting them. It helps to make the audience feel like participants rather than spectators, and to see the singers as characters rather than performers.

It is not to be believed that Wagner put in all that work on those long orchestral inner parts, full as they are of expressive and imaginative detail, intending them not to be heard. And for them to be heard the orchestra must not be too loud; if it is they are submerged, and all we hear is a fat, neutral, homogenized sound. Wagner needs to be played with weight, but also with inner clarity – a combination which few conductors except the greatest seem able to achieve. Another reason why the orchestra must not be loud is that if it is it makes the singers unintelligible. In Wagner the words are important for the same reason as in any other form of drama. I never cease to be amazed by people who say they find a Wagner opera boring, and then reveal that they have not the remotest idea what any of the characters has been saying. (What do they expect – surely there can scarcely be any form of drama, or for that matter any spectator, to which the same would not apply?) Over and above this is the fact that, unlike other opera composers, Wagner was working in a composite expressive medium of which the words are an integral part. When they cannot be heard it is not only the coherence of the drama which suffers but that of the artistic medium itself.

This ultimate unity of words and music in Wagner means that the question of performing his operas in translation cannot, strictly speaking, arise. In other operas, for much of the time, the words are merely a vehicle for the tunes – which is why they can be so silly and repetitious and yet not spoil anything. In consequence if other words are substituted nothing of artistic importance is even changed, let alone lost. But of Wagner it would be as true to say that the notes are vehicles for the words as the other way about. I showed on pages 20–22 how the most elaborate series of modulations would be not merely associated with but actually meaningful in terms of the words on which they occur. And not only is every shade of instrumental colour and every harmony inter-related with a specific word: the very consonants and vowel sounds of the word itself are part of the expressive language, and Wagner deliberately cultivated a verse form that made them so. If, then, the words are changed in Wagner this constitutes not a translation but a transcription. I am not against this any more than I am against arranging Haydn symphonies for two pianos, or playing a Brandenburg concerto in whatever instruments happen to be lying around the house; in just the same way it can be fun, and very illuminating when the only alternative is nothing. But it is no longer the work, and a deep aesthetic incomprehension is involved in insisting that it is.

The fact that words and music interpenetrate as they do needs to inform the questions of dynamics and tempo we were considering earlier. Some otherwise very fine conductors are not as sensitive to this interdependence as they should be. Solti used to drown the singers, and the glorious blaze of orchestral sound he put up exhausted them – an exhaustion which could sometimes mar the later stages of a performance; only in more recent years has he mellowed. Böhm quite often goes too fast to allow the singers to give their words their full expression, and they even have to gabble slightly sometimes to keep up. Knappertsbusch often took things so slowly that they had to extend their vowel sounds beyond the point where they could impart any subtleties of dramatic inflection to the words. (I regard the upper and lower limits of acceptable tempo in Wagner as being the points beyond which the words can no longer be given full value.) Karajan deliberately sacrifices verbal inflections to evenness of tone, and gets the singers to produce sounds of such purity as to have almost no dramatic implications – in effect he plays the operas as if they were nothing but music, gigantic symphonic poems for voices and orchestra. The results are more beautiful than I can believe anyone else has ever made Wagner sound, and yet still a whole dimension of the work is missing. The best Wagner is not the Wagner with the best sound. This music needs to sound less beautiful than it can.

In just the same way Wagner singing needs to be dramatic and musical in equal proportions, and the best Wagner singers are not necessarily those who produce the loveliest sounds. Kirsten Flagstad and Franz Völker, rather like Karajan, made such beautiful music one simply gloried in it and forgot about everything else. Nevertheless it is significant that one more often remembers these singers as themselves than in their roles. But it is great *performances* that constitute Wagner singing at its best, and this involves powers of vocal characterization and acting, gifts of psychological and dramatic insight, as well as beautiful singing: I personally think of Ludwig Weber's Gurnemanz and Gustav Neidlinger's Alberich, of Hans Hotter in his prime as Wotan, and Birgit Nilsson in hers as Brünnhilde, of Gottlob

Frick's Hagen, Norman Bailey's Sachs, Derek Hammond Stroud's Beckmesser. Likewise with conductors: Karajan makes everything sound marvellous but he does not serve the work, and my more specially treasured performances are Furtwängler's *Tristan*, Bruno Walter's *Walküre*, Solti's *Ring*, Knappertsbusch's *Parsifal*, Kempe's *Parsifal* and *Mastersingers*, Goodall's *Mastersingers* and *Götterdämmerung*. My greatest regret is that I never heard Toscanini, and that he left only a handful of snippety extracts on the old 78 rpm records. The most knowledgeable Wagnerians I know of, from Ernest Newman down, have tended to agree that the best performances they have ever heard were those of Toscanini at Bayreuth, which I mentioned earlier in this chapter.

Because of the scale of Wagner's works the long-playing record has benefited him proportionately more than any other composer. It has put his acts in the same relation to the length of a playing side as symphonic movements were to the old 78s. During the half-century that the 78 *was* the gramophone record we thought having to turn it over two or three times during a movement a small price to pay for the difference it made to our lives. But symphonies were about the biggest musical forms whose coherence could survive these circumstances. Wagner's works were practically out of the question. As John Culshaw has written in his book *Ring Resounding*:

"If anyone had tried to put *The Ring* on 78 rpm discs, the complete work would have required something like two hundred and twenty-four sides, or one hundred and twelve records. You would have been interrupted thirty-five times in *Rheingold* and over seventy times in *Götterdämmerung*; and most of the breaks would have made musical nonsense. Now, with the reasonable latitude provided by modern dubbing techniques, one can accommodate the whole of *Rheingold* on six sides, *Walküre* and *Siegfried* on ten sides each, and *Götterdämmerung* on twelve, making nineteen records for the entire cycle, which has a playing time of over fourteen hours."

So the long-playing record has made Wagner's works available to the gramophone for the first time. And they are being outstandingly well served. Each of the four *Ring* operas mentioned above by Mr Culshaw won the *Grand Prix du Disque Mondial* as the best recording of the year in which it appeared; and of the whole work *The Times* critic wrote in 1967: "It is quite certainly the outstanding single achievement in the annals of gramophone record-making." The *Götterdämmerung* is regarded by many people as the best recording ever made of anything – *The Gramophone* called it "the greatest achievement in gramophone history yet", and *Records and Recording* said "Nothing like this *Götterdämmerung* has ever before come out of the recording

studio." But most important of all has been its effect
on people's appreciation of Wagner. The music
critic of *The Financial Times* wrote: "Not since my
student days have I felt so passionately about the
Ring as after hearing this new *Götterdämmerung*. By
the end one is overwhelmed – and questioning all
the standards by which one thinks and works and
lives." During the last twenty years far more people
must have heard Wagner's operas on record than
have ever seen them in the opera house. There is no
doubt that this is one of the main reasons for the
enormous growth of interest in them that is now
taking place.

All the aspects of Wagner performance we have
considered so far in this chapter can be got on to a
gramophone record, but of course this is not the
whole work: there is all the visual side – the staging,
sets, costumes, lighting, acting. And this, like the
music, is on an unparalleled scale. I cannot understand people who say it does not matter all that
much. Only in live performance are the works
actually themselves. As the last chapter showed,
putting them on the stage has brought about some
of the most important developments in the history
of the theatre. If Wagner had thought it unimportant
he could have promoted concert performances and
not wasted several years of his maturity on the her-
culean labour of getting a special theatre built. The
trouble is that staged performances require such

combinations of talent, resources, money and time
that even moderately good results are a splendid
achievement. Inadequate results are the rule rather
than the exception. In provincial opera houses I
have seen performances that are literally excruciat-
ing. Perhaps it is this sort of thing that tempts
people to stay at home with those marvellous recordings and tell themselves they are not missing
anything.

Like all great dramas, Wagner's works have been
staged in countless different ways. I have not yet
heard of a *Ring* in modern dress but no doubt I shall
see it one day. I welcome every new attempt – and
though I may often judge the result a failure I shall
rarely say it should not have been tried. The only
kind of production that seems to me inherently
doomed is a compromise between different visions
of a work. The first postwar productions at Bayreuth, using no props, no scenery and only the
plainest costumes, revealed the universality of these
operas in an entirely new way and were enormously
exciting, but their success was misunderstood in
some places, where one began to find elements of
imitative abstractionism spatchcocked into romantic productions. The most perverse of these contained every naturalistic detail except the ones de-
manded by the text, so that over and again in an
otherwise realistic production something would
happen like Siegfried saying "What's that enormous

hat you're wearing?" to a bareheaded character.
The result was not only risible but precluded any
serious emotional involvement in the work.

Too many producers undertake to stage these
works without really knowing them – and works of
this calibre, complexity and depth take a lot of getting to know. A producer cannot just confine his
attention to stage requirements and leave the conductor to provide the music, because the drama is
centred in the music, and therefore the score is the
most, not the least, important thing for him to
know. Acting and stage movement in Wagner
constitute the outward behaviour of characters
whose inner feelings are being articulated in the
music. It must intimately relate to them and be
shaped by them but almost never fully express or
reveal them, and quite often must conflict with
them. The exploration of the relationship between
inner and outer is fundamental to this art, and it is
made impossible if the two are presented as the same
– if the characters merely "act out" the music. This
has the further result of making the stage movement
uncannily slow. Emotional deliberation, or absorp-
tion, or expansion, are very much slower processes
than physical actions – especially violent actions –
and since they are what this art is about its dramatic
pace, and hence the pulse of the music, is also very
much slower than action. If the producer makes the
mistake of giving the physical action not just a rela-

ted tempo but the *same* tempo the actors are made to move as if they were living in transparent treacle or under water, and the whole thing becomes eerily dreamlike. The key to Wagnerian acting, as to musical performance, lies in finding the right tempo, and that is one which relates organically to the music and yet appears natural and spontaneous.

The kind of Wagner production I most want to see now is one that does literally what Wagner asks for. The scores themselves contain detailed instructions about acting. For instance in a wordless passage of 57 bars in Act I of *Walküre* Wagner has written over the first eight: "For a while Sieglinde stands undecided, deliberating"; and over the next eight: "then slowly she turns with hesitant steps towards the door"; over the next eleven and a half: "there she stops again and stands lost in thought, with her face half turned away"; the next six and a half: "with quiet deliberation she opens the cupboard, fills a drinking horn and then sprinkles some herbs into it from a box"; the next four: 'having done this she looks round to catch the eye of Siegmund, who is watching her all the time"; and over the next two: "she becomes aware of Hunding watching them, and she starts towards the bedroom"; over the next twelve: "on the threshold she turns again, looks longingly at Siegmund and points with her eyes – persistently and with eloquent accuracy – to a spot on the trunk of the ashtree"; over the next two:

"Hunding starts up and gestures her roughly from the room"; and over the next three: "with a last glance at Siegmund she disappears into the bedroom and shuts the door behind her". .

Not only is this sort of thing contained in the scores. When Wagner saw his works in rehearsal and performance he naturally wanted to make changes, and he wrote down a lot of revised instructions. The best known are for *The Flying Dutchman*, which not only give bar-by-bar directions for the acting of some scenes but also change some of the tempi. Of course the trouble with all this is that whereas great nineteenth-century music still sounds great, great nineteenth-century acting now looks ridiculous. I can well believe that if Wagner's instructions were carried out to the letter the results in one or two places (e.g. "With the *molto piu animato* he can scarcely control himself any longer: he sings with fiery, utmost passion; and at the words 'Allmächtiger, durch diese sei's!' he flings himself on his knees") might be too hammy for modern tastes. But I am not entirely sure. I suspect that a really gifted producer who started out *wanting* to do everything Wagner's way would need to ignore very few of his instructions, and possibly none.

Similarly with his scenery and his stage directions. Whether it would be possible actually to have Fricka arrive on the scene at the beginning of Act II of *Walküre* in "a chariot drawn by two rams" I do not know, but if not there are comparatively few such stage directions, and the rest could certainly be carried out by someone determined to do so. The result would be a scenically spectacular *Ring*, and inevitably also a revelatory one, even if it led us to the conclusion that we can no longer accept Wagner's works when staged in Wagner's way. Of course it might lead us to the conclusion that this is the right way to do them. After all Wagner, like Shakespeare, was not a solitary genius, nor an academic, but a jack of all trades in the working theatre. He was a pro. And one reason why he made his instructions so detailed is that he knew what he was talking about.

Other Panthers For Your Enjoyment

Not Only for Students . . .

☐ **Chaucer (in modern prose by David Wright)**   **THE CANTERBURY TALES**   40p
The best version available. 'In Mr. Wright's modern English the tales become pure story-telling without losing the flavour of the oldest of English writers' – *The Bookman*. And *Tribune* adds: 'Mr. Wright can be as coarse as Chaucer'.

☐ **(translated by David Wright)**   **BEOWULF**   25p
Our only epic poem, and perhaps the earliest considerable poem in any modern language; it brings the doom-laden society of 6th century Anglo-Saxondom to glowing life. Wright's translation surpasses even William Morris's.

☐ **Frederick Engels**   **THE CONDITION OF THE WORKING CLASS IN ENGLAND**   40p
The modern world in all its facets was born 150 years ago in England. This is the classic account of that harsh birth.

☐ **D. E. Jones**   **INTRODUCTION TO PSYCHOLOGY**   50p
'This is the best introductory text I have read – simple terms and simple sentence construction, supported by examples from everyday life. If you are new to the field, here is your first book' – *Housecraft*

☐ **J. W. B. Douglas**   **THE HOME AND THE SCHOOL**   40p
Dr. Douglas's famous study of 5,000 boys and girls through their primary school years is essential reading for teachers and parents and all who are concerned with education. The conclusion begins to emerge that the success of a child's school career is much more connected with his home background, his social background, than it is with his original brightness.

☐ **J. W. B. Douglas and others**   **ALL OUR FUTURE**   40p
This important sequel to THE HOME AND THE SCHOOL takes the study of the 5,000 boys and girls from their eleventh to their fifteenth years, and the earlier book's suggestion – that not so much intelligence but social background ensures academic success – is reinforced. Both books have been recommended as basic reading by Unesco's *Bulletin of the International Bureau of Education*

Great Lives

☐ Antonia Fraser   MARY QUEEN OF
SCOTS   90p

The most acclaimed biography in years, and an international
bestseller. 700 pages, 16 pages of illustrations. 'Full of romance,
violence, intrigue' – *Newsweek*. 'This biography has long been
needed' – *The Scotsman*. 'Antonia Fraser has a high feeling for the
central tragedy' – *Sunday Times*

☐ Elizabeth Longford   WELLINGTON:
The Years of the Sword   75p

'Lady Longford has aimed to use every document, military,
political and personal, which illuminates Wellington the man. She
certainly did and to excellent effect. We can see Wellington in every
setting and can understand him better than before. A fine
achievement, giving as it does a rounded and profound portrait' –
Times Literary Supplement

☐ John B. Wolf   LOUIS XIV   75p

Glittering portrait of Louis, the Sun King, known as an absolute
ruler of France, and as profligate in his private life. 'A fair and
balanced portrait' – *The Observer*. 'The comprehensive picture of a
perpetual pageant of ceremonies, bonfires, fireworks, Te Deums,
revelry and what-have-you devised by one of the greatest showmen
who ever lived' – *Michael Foot, Evening Standard*

☐ translated and introduced by   THE MEMOIRS OF
David Cairns   OF BERLIOZ   £1

By the composer of *Symphonie Fantastique* and *The Damnation of
Faust* – the towering account of France's stormy Romantic
movement and of his own triumphs and defeats. A must for
musicians, historians and, perhaps above all, anyone looking for a
great and passionate life story.

Obtainable from all booksellers and newsagents. If you have
any difficulty please send purchase price plus 6p postage per
book to Panther Cash Sales, P.O. Box 11, Falmouth, Cornwall.

I enclose a cheque/postal order for titles ticked above plus 6p
a book to cover postage and packing.

Name...

Address ....

....